CITY
SECRETS
Rome

Robert Kahn
series editor

The Little Bookroom
New York

Series Editor: Robert Kahn
Editors: Angela Hederman and Pablo Conrad
Book and map design: Red Canoe, Deer Lodge TN, US
                      Caroline Kavanagh and Deb Koch

The editors acknowledge with appreciation Sergio Bregante, Susan
Bromberg, Fiona Duff, Lawrence, Jane, and Thomas Kahn, Alvin
Mesnikoff, Harriet McCurk, Stefanie Silverman, and Piero Villanelli.

Cover and divider page illustrations: from *The Complete Encyclopedia of
Illustration* by J.G. Heck
Endpaper photograph: Fototeca Unione, American Academy in Rome

The passage on Tasso's Oak that appears on page 187 from *Rome,
A Literary Companion* by John Varriano appears with the permission
of St. Martin's Press. The Latin inscriptions on pages 159 and 164 by
Paul Pascal copyright © 1988 by The New York Times Co. Reprinted
by permission.

First Printing: March 2000
Printed in Hong Kong by South China Printing Company (1988) Ltd.

Library of Congress Cataloging-in-Publication Data
Kahn, Robert, 1950–
City Secrets—Rome / Robert Kahn
p. cm.
ISBN 1-892145-04-9 (hardcover)
1. Art, Italian—Italy—Rome Guidebooks. 2. Art—Italy—Rome
Guidebooks. 3. Architecture—Italy—Rome Guidebooks. 4. Rome (Italy)
Guidebooks. I. Title. II. Title: Rome
N6920.K35 1999
914.5´63204929—dc21   99-38181
                                   CIP

Published by The Little Bookroom
5 St. Luke's Place
New York NY 10014
(212) 691-3321
(212) 691-2011 fax
editorial@citysecrets.com
www.citysecrets.com

HOW TO USE THIS BOOK

This is a highly subjective guidebook, reflecting the personal visions of our respondents. Our contributors were asked to recommend an overlooked or underappreciated work, or, alternatively, one that is well-known but about which they had a fresh insight, personal observation, little-known narrative, etc. Contributors were also asked to describe strolls, neighborhoods, events, shops, and all manner of idiosyncratic and traditional ways of spending time in a city.

These items have been organized into eleven zones, or areas of Rome. Each area (with the exception of Outside the City) has an accompanying map, keyed to the text by numbers. The numbers appear in oval lozenges **6.21** and include an item number and a map number (which is also the chapter number). For example, a lozenge with the number 6.21 denotes item number 21 from Chapter 6, which appears on Map 6.

In addition, two icons appear throughout the book to quickly help the reader find restaurants ✕ and shops ▥.

Many entries also are accompanied by recommended readings, which refer the reader to a bibliography beginning on page 240.

ACCESS TO CLOSED SITES

For permission to visit sites that are normally closed, you must obtain a written permit and book the date and time of your visit in advance. Apply to the Comune di Roma, Ripartizione X, Piazza Campitelli 7, ☎ 06 67 10 20 70; fax 06 67 10 31 18. It is best to deliver a written request in person and then follow up with a phone call to set an appointment.

Every care has been take to ensure the accuracy of the information in this book. However, the publisher is not able to accept responsibility for any consequences arising from use of the guide or the information it contains.

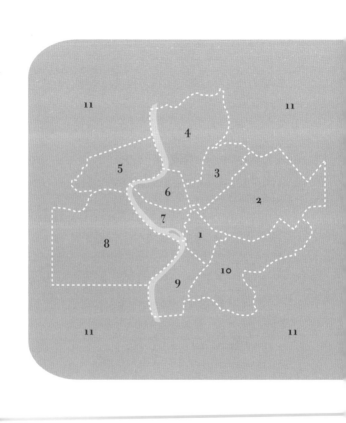

contents

preface

I once spent nearly an hour haggling over a box of Cuban cigars in the Porta Portese flea market. I could not have been prouder when the dealer came down from $250 to $150, but it was still far too expensive for a young architect living on borrowed money in Rome. An elderly local watching the transaction winked at me, then walked up to the seller and exchanged what seemed to be no more than five words. After paying a mere $75 for the same cigars, he smiled and pushed me back toward the table to try again. I called on my best Italian, "Whatever the signor said, goes for me, too."

This seems to me the best way to experience a city: move there and surround yourself with the people who know it best. The second best way is to ask the people who have done that to share their wisdom. That is the idea of this book.

The contributors include some of America's foremost cultural figures—from learned specialists to eccentric generalists—all with an intriguing personal vision. Their recommendations cover the entire city, ranging from insightful commentary on well-known sights and artwork to the revelation of secret discoveries and special places. This book is intended as a companion to general guidebooks. Therefore we have compiled only personal favorites of these distinguished people.

Like the Romans, these experts have lived with and among the city's treasures. The buildings, paintings, sculpture, and places exist not only as a connection to the distant past but as a living part of everyday activity.

To appreciate them more fully, it is necessary to observe that singular experience which is Roman daily life. I can think of no better advice than to allow yourself the leisure of exploring an unknown street, of wandering into a neighborhood church, or staying far too long in an out-door café. In this way you catch a glimpse of the heart of this great city and discover something that you can call your own.

ROBERT KAHN
New York City

Robert Kahn is an architect in private practice. His work has been widely published. He has taught design, most recently at Yale University. In 1981 he was awarded the Prix de Rome by the American Academy in Rome. He lives and works in New York.

THE CAPITOLINE,

THE FORUM

AND

THE PALATINE

1

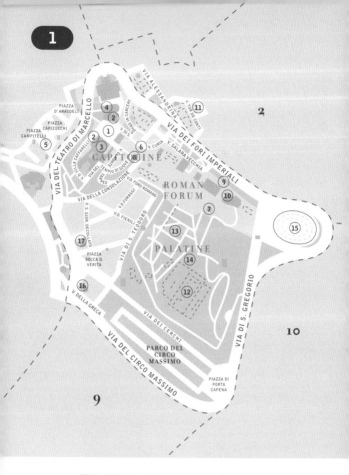

THE CAPITOLINE

1.1 Piazza del Campidoglio

Michelangelo, 1539–1592; completed by Giacomo Della Porta

Perhaps the most perfect public space ever built—a marvel of harmony and elegance.
Theodore K. Rabb
Historian, Princeton University

The center of ancient and modern Rome. By climbing the sloping *cordonata* one escapes the deafening traffic noise of a bustling modern city to be transported through time, first to Michelangelo's Renaissance and then to ancient Rome. Here stood the Temple of Capitoline Jove; nearby the sybil appeared to Augustus Caesar announcing the coming of a greater king. Michelangelo has recreated the ancient center, clothing it in a thoroughly modern architecture. From this perfect platform—an outdoor room—one looks down upon the ancient Forum and into the distant past.
William E. Wallace
Art historian, Washington University

The Capitol enjoys, like a Japanese mountain shrine, the drama of arrival and the reward of adorned space. Come from any direction, through all the seasons, all times of day, and all celebrations of place. I suppose no plaza in the Western world holds more substance for me.
James R. Turner
Landscape architect

Refined combination of place-making, architecture, urban intervention, and sculpture. Inspiring and memorable. A singular architectural achievement.
Charles Gwathmey
Architect

Earliest and best example of modern urbanism. Michelangelo's paving pattern was compelling enough to have been installed 400 years later in exact accordance with the original drawing.
George E. Hartman
Architect

THE FORUM

VIEW

One's first sight of the Forum should be from the Capitoline Hill. From the Piazza del Campidoglio walk to the left of the Palazzo Senatorio along via San Pietro in Carcere. As Fredrika Bremer wrote, "I came to the Capitol and looked down the other side. There before my eyes opened an immense grave, and out of the grave rose a city of monuments in ruin...it was the giant apparition of ancient Rome."

PAMELA KEECH
Sculptor, installation artist, historian

Visit the piazza at night, around midnight (but not Friday or Saturday). Rome is magical always but in a special way at night. Georgina Masson (see p. 242) was certainly right about this piazza—it's the nexus point where ancient and modern intersect, and illuminated at night, with Michelangelo on one side of the Palazzo Senatorio, and the Forum, the Colosseum, etc., on the other, the experience is haunting.

DAVID MAYERNIK
Architect and fresco painter

ALSO RECOMMENDED BY
MARK ADAMS, GERALDINE ERMAN, LAWRENCE FANE, URSULA HEIBGES, FRANK HOLMES, JOHN KEARNEY, PETER KOMMERS, ROGER MARTIN, DAVID PISCUSKAS, ERNST PULGRAM, ANTON RAJER, JEFFERY RUDELL, JON MICHAEL SCHWARTING, PETER SCHWEITZER, PAMELA STARR

RECOMMENDED READING 56

1.2 Capitoline Museum (Palazzo Nuovo and Palazzo Conservatori)

Piazza del Campidoglio

Above all, see the Capitoline Museum, when it's open on Saturday evening. The perfect place to begin a tour of Rome,

as Georgina Masson taught me to do long ago.
JOSEPH CONNORS
Art historian, Columbia University

The Capitoline Museums are admittedly Renaissance but
built near the 1st-century Tabularium, the state archive of
ancient Rome. The collections of antiquities are superb.
The name refers to the discovery of a human head around
500 bc at the foundation of the Temple of Jupiter, an omen
that Rome would one day be the Caput Mundi.
ELAINE FANTHAM
Classicist, Princeton University

ALSO RECOMMENDED BY
MARY J. AND BRIAN CURRAN, THOMAS H. WATKINS

1.3 Palazzo dei Conservatori

Fasti Triumphales, epigraphical fragments from the Arch of Augustus

19 BC

...emotion at reading the names of the triumphators in suc-
cession from Romulus.
R. ROSS HOLLOWAY
Archaeologist, Brown University

Statue of Marcus Aurelius

161–180 AD

One of the few remaining equestrian bronzes from antiquity;
right setting (Michelangelo sited it).
PETER J. HOLLIDAY
*Historian of classical art and archaeology, California State
University–Long Beach*

ALSO RECOMMENDED BY
FRANK HOLMES

The Capitoline Wolf

Probably Etruscan, 6th–5th century BC

She may not look very fierce—or maternal—but the archaic

stylization, abstraction, and taut intensity of the She Wolf appeal to modern sensibilities. The fact that the human babies (Romulus and Remus) nursing under her belly were added during the Renaissance makes it even better, if less consistent. Clearly the meanings attached to this life-size bronze statue have changed over time, but that seems to me proof of its power and another example of the way one period in Roman history builds on another.

JAYNE MERKEL
Art historian and critic

Statue of Isis

120–138 AD

Isis is presiding over her own private ceremony. Her right hand holds the sistrum, the ancient Egyptian instrument for warding off evil and encouraging good; her left hand holds a pitcher containing sacred water from the Nile. Isis' importance originated in ancient Egypt and, regarded as a major goddess by the Romans, she found devotees throughout the entire Mediterranean world.

The statue is not intended to represent Isis herself, but most probably an empress or member of the royal family in her guise, for even in Egypt, and later in Rome, noblewomen affected her costume and attributes. This statue, carved in Luna marble, was found in Hadrian's Villa. It is certainly Roman, even though the sculptor's hand has been identified as Greek (by the carving and the struts). A voluminous Roman mantle completely conceals her figure; Egyptian representations show the female figure through diaphanous cloth. Isis and her priestesses are identified by the fringed shawl tied with the so-called Isis knot, or by the sistrum and pitcher. They often wear the *uraeus* on the headdress, as does this statue. The goddess of fertility and rebirth, Isis is often depicted nursing her infant son Horus.

NORMA GOLDMAN
Classicist, Wayne State University

1.4 ## Santa Maria in Aracoeli

Piazza d'Aracoeli

This is best at Christmas: gypsy princesses carry the Santo Bambino to the presepio, or model crèche scene, as Abruzzo shepherds play bagpipes.

MARY J. CURRAN AND BRIAN A CURRAN
Costume historian; Art historian, Pennsylvania State University

RECOMMENDED READING 1, 18, 38, 64, 69, 103, 105, 109

VIEW

THE FORUM FROM THE CAPITOLINE

Climb up the ramp to the Campidoglio on a moonlit night (avoiding the cruising area by the Tarpeian Rock unless this is your interest) and take the road down to the right, until the panorama opens out at your feet. This is where it all began, after all, in Iron Age times, and it was probably beautiful then, too.
INGRID D. ROWLAND
Historian, University of Chicago

1.5 ## Vecchia Roma

✗ Piazza Campitelli 18, ☎ 06 68 64 604

You have one evening to spend on the best meal of your life. I recommend Vecchia Roma. The cuisine is superb, the ambience beautiful (especially if you sit outside), the surroundings are medieval/Renaissance Rome.
PAMELA STARR

Always great; eat outside if possible. The service is superb and the roast goat shouldn't be missed.
PETER G. ROLLAND

Quite well-known, but don't let its popularity keep you away from this terrific restaurant. In the fall, I suggest the tagliatelle with white truffles and lemon. Unbelievable.
DAVID ST. JOHN

ALSO RECOMMENDED BY
KIMBERLY ACKERT, THOMAS L. BOSWORTH, CAREN CANIER, CHARLES K. WILLIAMS II

THE FORUM

The center of life in ancient Rome.
JAMES S. ACKERMAN
Art historian, Harvard University

If you get there just as it opens, you can have some time alone with the monuments.
CELIA SCHULTZ
Classicist, Bryn Mawr College

I try to think of the Roman Forum as a government center very gradually growing up around a flat open-ground meeting place. Start with a piazza, a market square, add loggias to get in out of the rain. Build basilicas as year-round meeting places, then go from there as cult centers and specialized structures (Senate, Tabularium, etc.) are articulated. The interior of the Senate gives you some access to the ideal re-creation of what it was like, as do the churches along the city-side edge. You get a sense of the streets from walking inside Trajan's market.
JAMES H.S. MCGREGOR
Professor of comparative literature, University of Georgia

I still believe this is one of the best introductions to Rome, to an understanding of the resonance of history as it is artic-ulated again and again throughout the city as a whole—that intoxicating mix of the ancient and timeless with the recent. The Forum is startling, powerful, monumental, intimate, and always surprising.
DAVID ST. JOHN
Poet, University of Southern California

The most complicated of all Roman sites, which, with the proper guide, always comes to life and becomes the most intelligent mess I could ever imagine.
JAMES L. BODNAR
Architect

Atmosphere. Go there as I first did, on a slightly misty March morning.

R. Ross Holloway
Archaeologist, Brown University

ALSO RECOMMENDED BY
Frances Blank, Anna Blume, Mary J. and Brian Curran, Katherine Geffcken, Catherine Spotswood Gibbes, Lynn Kearney, Susan Kleinberg, Benjamin Kohl, David Konstan, John C. Leavey, Anton Rajer, Rocío Rodríguez, Michele Renee Salzman, H. Alan Shapiro, Susan Silberberg-Peirce, John H. Thow, John Varriano

1.6 Arch of Septimius Severus

203 AD

The enormous letters on the attic form the largest surviving dedicatory inscription from antiquity. As you look up, remember that the letters were once gilded bronze, now mostly pried away. On the four larger panels on the columns (two on each side) carved reliefs depict Severus' victories over the barbarians of Parthia (now Iran). In the middle panels one can see barbarian prisoners being led in chains. This was almost certainly the model for the Arch of Constantine that stands next to the Colosseum, and which was built more than 100 years later.

Richard Brilliant
Art historian and archaeologist, Columbia University

1.7 Arch of Titus

81 AD

The Arch of Titus on the Forum contains relief carvings showing treasures taken from the Temple in Jerusalem. Roman Jews today never pass under this arch.

Rudolf Arnheim
Art historian, University of Michigan

ALSO RECOMMENDED BY
J. Richard Judson

Through Hawthorne's
The Marble Faun

For this walk I would have in hand a copy
of Nathaniel Hawthorne's romance *The
Marble Faun*. I would begin at the bottom
of the stepped ramp or *cordonata* which
leads up to the Capitoline Hill or
Campidoglio. At the top and with the statue
of Marcus Aurelius in front of me, I would
turn left and go into the Palazzo Capitolino
which houses two floors of ancient statuary.
Upon entering, climb the grand staircase
and proceed into the room straight ahead—
the Sala del Galata Morente or the Room
of the Dying Gaul. At this moment I would
open *The Marble Faun* to Chapter 1 and
read the first paragraph in which Hawthorne
describes this sublime warrior in his death
swoon. The marble statue is a Roman copy
of the original bronze from the school of
Pergamon dating from the 3rd to the 2nd
century BC. I am not so interested, at this
moment, in the history of the statue as I am
in the spell that Hawthorne creates as one
reads his lines. Then proceed to the window
in the same room that overlooks the Roman
Forum and beyond. Read the next paragraph: "From one of the windows of this
salon, we may see...." What he describes is
the same now as it was then: the foundation
of the Capital, the Arch, the Forum, the
domes of Christian churches, the sweep of
the Colosseum beyond. So much history
"heaped into the intervening space" from

ITINERARY

a *cordonata*,
The Capitoline

b Capitoline Museum,
Room of the Dying
Gaul

the place where one stands at the window
to the landscape beyond. The moment
and the read are spellbinding. (Chapter 1,
Miriam, Hilda, Kenyon, Donatello)

Or, an alternative stroll

Read *The Marble Faun* in its entirety; then
go to the Dying Gaul, then the window. From
here proceed through the Sala di Fauno
to the great, middle *salone* in search of
Hawthorne's Marble Faun. This being is
hard to track down as there are many fauns
in the room. (Georgina Masson places
Hawthorne's faun in the room with the
Dying Gaul, but, to my mind, it is neither
there nor in the Sala di Fauno. The faun in
the large *salone* is much more consistent
with Hawthorne's description.) Read carefully and you will find this creature, or in
the words of Hawthorne: "Neither man nor
animal, yet no monster, but a being in whom
both races meet on friendly ground," and
"if the spectator broods long enough over
the statue, he will be conscious of its spell;
all the genial characteristics of creatures
that dwell in woods and fields, will seem
mingled and kneaded into one substance,
along with the kindred qualities in the
human soul.... The essence ... was compressed long ago, and still exists, within that
discolored marble surface of the Faun of
Praxiteles." (Chapter 1, Miriam, Hilda,
Kenyon, Donatello)

➤

There are many other places that one could go to follow the journey of Hawthorne's four individuals. Next for me would be the Church of the Cappuccini (Santa Maria della Concezione) at the bottom end of the via Vittorio Veneto. In the first chapel on the right one finds Guido Reni's great altarpiece *Saint Michael Trampling on the Devil*. Hawthorne's characters are very excited by this painting, which plays a significant role in the story's plot, and the book led me to a painting which I otherwise might not have contemplated so intently. The church itself is also a perfect setting for the peregrinations of Hawthorne's otherworldly and somewhat sinister foursome.

If this is not already enough I would now proceed to the Tarpeian Rock or Rupe Tarpeia. One gets there by following the via di Monte Tarpeio, a narrow alley, leading up to the foot of what is believed to be the Tarpeian Rock beneath the Palazzo Caffarelli on the back side of the Capitoline Hill. It is from this point that the Rock is best seen. Many a traitor to the Roman Republic leapt to his death from this bare cliff. And it was here, in a small courtyard that existed until 1868, that one of Hawthorne's characters meets a tragic death. This rock also captured the imagination of Virgil, who refers to it in the *Aeneid*, and Milton writes about it in *Paradise Regained*.

JUDITH DIMAIO
Architect, Yale University

RECOMMENDED READING 39, 46

1.8   ## The Rostrum

from 338 BC

An important inspirational center surrounded by the archaeological fragments of the Roman world, both Republican
and Imperial. A special place for contemplation.
THOMAS L. BOSWORTH
Architect, University of Washington

1.9   ## Four maps of the Roman Empire

Mussolini, 1932
via dei Fori Imperiali

I love to stand before these maps of marble and gaze awe-
struck at the grandeur that was the Roman Empire, its vast
extent, and weep at its fall, with nostalgia for the loss. The
first shows Rome's dominion in the 8th century BC; the second as it has expanded in 146 BC, after the Punic Wars; then
in 14 AD, after the death of Augustus; and finally as it looked
under Trajan, in 98–117 AD, covering North Africa and up
into Britain, and east to Turkey.
ALEXANDER GORLIN
Architect

RECOMMENDED READING 18, 29, 60, 69, 83, 86

1.10   ## Santa Francesca Romana

9th century; 17th-century façade
Sacristy opens at 4:30 p.m.

Icon of the Virgin and Child

Artist unknown, late 6th or early 7th century

One of the few icons surviving from this period and typically
Roman in style. Though often photographed, to be in the actual
presence of this painting is an almost spiritual experience.
JOHN KENFIELD
Archaeologist and art historian, Rutgers University

THE PALATINE

The strongest echoes of Roman antiquity are here, uncompromised by contemporary intrusion. From the Palatine, great panoramas of Rome can be seen including monuments of later eras. Early in the morning, before other tourists arrive, one can enjoy the Palatine undisturbed. The effect is hypnotic and undiminished by familiarity.

STEVEN BROOKE
Architectural photographer and writer

ALSO RECOMMENDED BY
MELISSA MEYER, PAMELA STARR

1.11 TERRACE RESTAURANT AT THE HOTEL FORUM

via Tor de'Conti 25, at via Madonna dei Monti
☎ 06 67 92 446

VIEW

The terrace incorporates a medieval bell tower; it overlooks the center of the Roman Forum with the Colosseum off to the left and Piazza Venezia to the right. In between, Caesar's Forum, the Forum of Augustus, the Capitoline Hill with its buildings ancient, medieval, and modern. The massive medieval Torre dei Segni and Nerva's colonnacce all crowd beneath you. Even for a veteran Romanista, it's enough to take your breath away. On a moonlit night, adjourn to the terrace of the Campidoglio that overlooks the Forum and see it all in moonglow. Edith Wharton's great story "Roman Fever" was surely set right here.
INGRID D. ROWLAND

1.12 House of Augustus

Frescoes, 25 BC–25 AD

The House of Augustus on the Palatine Hill was not discovered until the early 1960s. It is of historical importance as the relatively modest house of the first emperor, and the fact that its remains show its joint residential/official function. My favorite aspect of the monument is the Room of the Masks in which all four walls of fresco are still intact. They depict small-scale theater backdrops (*scaena frons*) in vibrant colors that may have decorated a small private theater. Unfortunately, it's difficult to obtain a *permesso*, but most worthwhile.

Thomas Gordon Smith
Architect, University of Notre Dame

1.13 ## Farnese Gardens

16th century

Visit the upper gardens of the Palatine on a spring day—the smell of stone and freshly raked leaves and cool shade are unforgettable.

Gianne Harper
Artist and painter

1.14 ## Nero's Cryptoporticus

This underground passage—cool, damp, and dark—carries you deep into memory from the Palatine's Farnese Gardens (16th century) overlooking the Forum, back into the Roma Quadrata where primitive Roman civilization began, where you find the birthplace of Romulus and Remus and the ilex-covered remains of the Temple of Cybele, the Asia Minor fertility goddess worshiped in that spot through the ages. A favorite place for dreaming about Roman history and enjoying picnics—the picnics now forbidden! Could the Cryptoporticus have carried Freud to his now famous analogy between the human mind and the Palatine in which he proposes the process of ruin, disintegration, and reconstruction both in the mind and the ancient city as a way of allowing room for everything in the inexorable process of growth? Visiting the Palatine, indeed visiting Rome itself (the Palatine being an emblem for the city), you have the experience of the continuum of space and time—especially at the moment you come up out of the Cryptoporticus and

find yourself standing among the most alluring remains of
ruin, disintegration, and reconstruction in the world.
JANET SULLIVAN
Writer, Rhode Island School of Design

NEAR THE FORUM

1.15 ## The Colosseum

Emperors Vespasian and Titus, 79–80 AD

The single most impressive monument in the city is the
Colosseum. While the last gladiatorial combats and staged
animal hunts ended in the 5th and 6th centuries, the ruins
of the great stone ellipse still stand, damaged by a series of
earthquakes and by its use as a quarry for later builders, but
still a triumph of engineering. The huge travertine blocks of
the exterior were once held in place by metal butterfly
clamps that had been inserted in holes filled with lead, all
later dug out to be recycled by the metal-poor people of the
Middle Ages and early Renaissance, giving the Colosseum
its present pitted appearance. But the clamps were hardly
needed: the great blocks of travertine on the exterior are
held together by their own weight in "dry wall construction"
without any mortar. The same is true of the inner piers of
volcanic tufa. The exterior travertine and inner marble
seats were plundered to provide materials for the steps of
St. Peter's and for the Palazzo della Cancelleria, among
other buildings. If you visit in the summer, bear in mind
that the spectators (up to 50,000) were shielded from the
sun under a vast awning called the *velarium* that was suspended by ropes from 240 masts distributed around the
upper story. The projecting stone corbels, which contain
the sockets for these masts, can still be seen. For a better
sense of what it was like for spectators, attend a soccer game
at the Olympic Stadium late in the season when emotions
are running high.
NORMA GOLDMAN
Classicist, Wayne State University

A new visitor to Rome should go first to the Colosseum.
Since it is said that Rome will stand as long as the
Colosseum stands, and the world will last as long as Rome
stands, it would be good to check first that everything is in
order with the universe.
VIRGINIA L. BUSH
Art historian

This building seems to set the scale for the grandness of
Rome found in the rest of the city. The arches predict the
vaults and domes of the future Baroque architecture.
MARJORIE KREILICK
Artist, University of Wisconsin

ALSO RECOMMENDED BY
FRANCES BLANK, ANDREA CALLARD, LESLIE RAINER

RECOMMENDED READING 26, 60, 81, 95, 97

1.16 ## Santa Maria in Cosmedin

8th century; rebuilt 12th century
Piazza della Bocca della Verità

I know of no other structure in Rome that so conveys the
roots of religiosity that finds such grandiose expression in
the many later churches in Rome. In this simple, spare
medieval church, paved in splendid Cosmati mosaic, one
feels the mystery of darkness and the hopefulness of light
as nowhere else.
JEFFREY SCHIFF
Artist

1.17 ## Church and Oratory of San Giovanni Decollato

1530s–1550s
(decorations of church continued until 1590)
Corner of via di San Giovanni Decollato and via
della Misericordia

San Giovanni Decollato, which is rarely mentioned in
guidebooks, was home to the Confraternity of San Giovanni
Decollato, a brotherhood of Florentine residents of Rome

including merchants, bankers, and artists—Antonio da Sangallo, Michelangelo, and Giorgio Vasari, to name just a few. (Upon Michelangelo's death in 1564 his body was carried from his home to Santi Apostoli by members of the Confraternity.)

The mission of this brotherhood was to comfort prisoners condemned to death during their final hours, accompany them to execution, and see to their burial—often in the cloister of San Giovanni Decollato. During the years of the Roman Inquisition many of the executions were of heretics, some of whom were priests and scholars—including Giordano Bruno, the former Dominican monk, philosopher, poet, and mnemonics advisor to Pope Pius V. A statue of Bruno now marks the spot in the Campo dei Fiori where he was burned alive.

The decorations, frescoes, and altarpieces in the church and oratory, done almost entirely by Florentine painters (including Francesco Salviati, Jacopino del Conte, and Giorgio Vasari, again to name just a few) not only present a stunning history of Mannerist painting from the 1530s to the 1590s, but can be seen, through the choice of subjects and the manner in which these subjects are depicted, to express and confirm the commitment and mission of the patrons.

I try to make a point of going on June 24, the Feast of Saint John the Baptist. After a ceremony in the church there is a candlelight procession in the cloister. A priest with a censer is followed by the *confratelli* dressed in their hooded black robes and the guests who then place their candles upon the stones marking the burial sites.

The ceremonies are followed by a reception. The premises are entirely open and lit making this a good opportunity to view the paintings in the church and oratory and to visit the *camera storica* where the *tavolette*, torches, and other objects used by the Confraternity are preserved.

JEAN WEISZ

Art historian, University of California—Los Angeles

THE ESQUILINE

2

2

3

1

COLOSSEUM

THE ESQUILINE

2.1 **Column of Trajan**

113 AD
via dei Fori Imperiali

For me, this is the finest single example of Roman art.
ROGERS V. SCUDDER
Schoolmaster (retired), Groton School

Important for its narrative history and great influence on
later monuments.
RICHARD BRILLIANT
Art historian and archaeologist, Columbia University

2.2 **Markets of Trajan**

Appollodorus of Damascus, 2nd century AD
via 4 Novembre

Often overlooked as people go scurrying about the Forum,
Trajan's Market was not only an urban renewal project to
get rid of the slums that crowded the edge of the fora but
was, in itself, the Rockefeller Center of ancient Rome.
Fascinating to wander through and to realize the mercantile,
engineering, and architectual skills of the Romans of that era.
BARRY LEWIS
Architectural historian

The quality of the Romans' dedication to urban life is best
seen in the market—for everyday use—rather than the temple.
ROBERT MCCARTER
Architect, University of Florida

The Markets of Trajan are one of Rome's best-preserved
ancient sites—hundreds of shops are virtually intact, and
the great Market Hall still has its magnificent vault. In this
respect, Trajan's Markets are quite different from other,
more ruined, places of ancient commerce, such as Ostia
Antica and Porticus Aemilia. At Ostia, the walls of the *tabernae*, or shops, are so worn down that they resemble a

shallow relief drawing on the surface of the earth. We perceive these ruins more with our mind than our senses—we reconstruct them the way we would decipher a map or schematic diagram. A visit to Trajan's Markets is a dramatically different experience. Here, massive walls rise to envelop us; cavernous roofs arch above our heads; narrow corridors lead us along meandering paths marked with shafts of sunlight and cast shadows. Here, more than anywhere else in Rome, we can experience the mass and body of ancient architecture.

Trajan's Markets once accommodated a myriad human transactions: buying, selling, haggling, arguing, raw jostling. They are now mostly silent. (Tourists rarely find their way here.) Yet as we walk through their varied spaces, we can envision the bustling activities of the marketplace, the loud calls of vendors, the vivid colors and odors that once filled the streets and narrow passageways. There are six floors in the market's great hemicycle: fruit and flowers were sold on the ground floor; the vaulted halls and arcades of the next floor housed oils and wines; exotic goods such as pepper and spices took up the third and fourth floors; the fifth floor housed offices for public assistance; on the sixth floor were fish ponds, some linked to an aqueduct that supplied fresh water, others connected to a saltwater line from Ostia.

Unlike the fora or the baths, Trajan's Markets were not designed as a formal, axial ensemble. Theirs is a thoroughly pragmatic and opportunistic planning strategy. Ruthlessly carved out of the hillside, the market spaces remain largely undecorated. Rows of small *tabernae* contrast with the large vaulted space of the Market Hall. Narrow curving streets are ingeniously nestled between the *exedra* of the Forum of Trajan and the Quirinal Hill. Strange, in-between alleys and stairways emerge unexpectedly like shrill calls in the marketplace. Mysterious hemispherical domed halls suggest purposeful assemblies of citizens. This great variety in sizes and shapes of spaces, as well as the dramatic shifts in floor levels, makes Trajan's Markets one of Rome's liveliest, least austere ruins.

SANDA D. ILIESCU
Artist, designer

2.3   **Papok**

Salita del Grillo 6b,   ☎ 06 69 92 21 83
closed Mondays

Excellent fish restaurant near Trajan's Forum.
GEORGE BISACCA

2.4   **The Domus Aurea / Nero's Golden House**

Severus and Celer, 64–68 AD
via Labicana 136, opposite the Colosseum
Admission by permit only
For permission and to arrange for a guide, call the
Soprintendenza Archeologica di Roma, Piazza S. Maria
Nova 53,   ☎ 06 69 90 110; fax 06 67 87 689

Gaining access to this site remains difficult, but the Domus
Aurea fully rewards the effort. The palace is both an architectural masterpiece, whose influence molded the very shape
of Imperial Rome, and an important primary source for
Neronian history. Its appeal, however, extends far beyond
the academic. Even the most jaded scholar must acknowledge
the Domus Aurea's powerful romantic pull: the most fabulous project of an emperor known for his flamboyance. The
experience becomes even more intense when one ventures
off the main route, into corridors that remain mostly unex-
cavated. A visitor easily might imagine himself among those
first Renaissance explorers, delving into the lost palace of a
legendary king. It is what every romantic knows archaeology
really ought to be like.
R.J.W. CRO
Art historian and archaeologist, Princeton University

This ruin is a microcosm of the Roman condition: invention
and delight within highly pragmatic constraints. As a buried
structure it offers the viewer a labyrinthine journey which
requires bodily labor and is accompanied by phenomenal
experiences of light and temperature changes. The memory
transferred lives under one's skin and is always accessible.
IAIN LOW
Architect

Paintings on the wall of the Domus Aurea

It made me cry to see these paintings crumbling before my
eyes, as if, as in a Fellini movie, seeing them was part of
their destruction.
JAMES L. BODNAR
Architect

ALSO RECOMMENDED BY
ANDREA CALLARD

2.5 San Pietro in Vincoli
Piazza di San Pietro in Vincoli 4a

Statue of Moses and Tomb of Julius II
Michelangelo, 1513–1516

Less famous and polished than the Pietà in St. Peter's, but
far more emotionally evocative. I am moved each time I come
upon this church and rediscover one of Michelangelo's
greatest treasures.
DANNY MEYER
Restaurateur

An extraordinary work of sculpture; powerful, personal,
terrible in its authority, and a symbol of the artist's ambition.
RICHARD BRILLIANT
Art historian and archaeologist, Columbia University

A wonderful tribute to the artistic taste and urge for
memorialization of the doughty old warrior pope, Julius II.
BENJAMIN KOHL
Historian, Vassar College

ALSO RECOMMENDED BY
JEROME M. COOPER, RICHARD FRANK, JOHN KEARNEY,
STUART M. MERTZ, HENRY MIRICK

2.6 Auditorium of Maecenas

late 1st century BC
Largo Leopardi at the junction of via Mecenate
and via Merulana

This little Augustan building was, for long years, difficult or
impossible to visit, but has recently been made accessible
with generous opening hours and is never crowded. The
official personnel, in fact, always seem just a bit surprised
to welcome a visitor, but they are *molto gentile*.

The building is situated in the neighborhood which was
once occupied by the fabulous Gardens of Maecenas and,
later, by the extended properties of Nero's Golden House. If
you leave the Colosseum square at the northwest corner, the
street names will give a sense of the ancient setting (viale
Domus Aurea, crossing the Parco Oppio, leads to the via
Mecenate, which debouches on the via Merulana just across
that thoroughfare from the *auditorio*). The park (in Latin,
horti) was established by C. Cilnius Maecenas, a very wealthy
Roman of Etruscan descent and Augustus' informal advisor
in matters of culture. A patron of both Virgil and Horace,
Maecenas was dedicatee of some Horatian odes and his park
is mentioned in one satire. Upon his death in 8 BC,
Maecenas' properties passed to Augustus by testament.

Roman architects loved to play with and challenge nature
in various ways. Towers, like the one in this same park from
which Nero traditionally is believed to have watched the fire
of 64 AD, placed their owners high in the clouds. (Horace,
at *Odes* 3.29, refers to Maecenas' *molem propinquam nubibus
arduis*, "structure near the steep clouds," which may well be
the same structure to which Suetonius refers.) The other
extreme is represented by subterranean or semisubterranean buildings. Along with the garden room of Livia's Villa
at Prima Porta (see p. 31), the *auditorio* is an example of the
latter.

The original structure of the *auditorio* probably dates from
the period of Maecenas' life though the visible ornament is
from the 1st century AD. The room is semisubterranean and
consists of a ramp descending into an apsidal room, with
wide steps ascending the apse. From the upper level of the

stepped area, one can look down on the white and red tiled mosaic floor (what remains of it) and painted walls with niches.

The common label of *auditorio* was given by the first scholarly investigators of the building, based on its shape. However, later discovery of the remains of water pipes in the upper part of the apse cast doubt on the identification of those wide steps as seating. Consequently the building is now labeled a summer nymphaeum/dining pavilion. Like the garden room of Livia's Villa at Prima Porta, the *auditorio* was probably another cool, semisubterranean summer retreat. But the mystery remains, as it does for the Temple of Minerva Medica, the Villa della Farnesina, and other examples of Roman urban leisure architecture that continue to entice and entrance by their liminal forms and locations.

LINDA W. RUTLAND GILLISON
Classicist, University of Montana

2.7 Agata e Romeo

✕ via Carlo Alberto 45, ☎ 06 44 66 115

This is one of the best restaurants in Rome for dinner. It's not inexpensive, but eminently worth it. Small and intimate, so be sure to make a reservation. It's situated conveniently near Stazione Termini and Santa Maria Maggiore.

PAMELA STARR

2.8 Church of Santa Prassede

Pope Pascal I, 817–824
via Santa Prassede 9A

The greatest surviving medieval Roman mosaic can be seen up close, in the dome, on the walls. Nobody ever urges visitors to go there.

JAMES S. ACKERMAN
Art historian, Harvard University

In dazzling, timeless fashion, the apse mosaic at Santa Prassede shows how to get things done in the Mediterranean world (and not only there). Jesus, attired in gold, stands at

the center, flanked by his trusted lieutenants Peter and Paul.
Each of these is presenting to him one of the holy sisters
Prassede and Pudenziana. On the viewer's left, Paul rests
one arm around the shoulders of Prassede and with the other
hand, extended and palm up, gestures as if to introduce her,
a client, to the chief patron. In a mirror image of this courtly
scene, on the right, Peter gives a similarly warm recommendation to Pudenziana. The words spoken are left to the
viewer's imagination.

LESTER K. LITTLE
*Professor of History, Smith College, Director of the American
Academy in Rome, August 1998 to present*

In the small vaulted chapel, one is literally inside the mosaics,
which completely engulf you. This is about as close as you'll
get to such radiance. The chapel also contains part of the
marble column from Christ's flagellation, later depicted by
Andrea Mantegna. The impressive mosaics of the chancel
arch show Christ surrounded by six saints, with twelve lambs
floating above.

KENNETH FRAZELLE
*Composer, North Carolina School of the Arts, Composer-in-
Residence for the Los Angeles Chamber Orchestra*

The 9th-century mosaics of the apse are a splendid program
of saints and Bible passages, now seen to be directly inspired
by the event of the consecration of the church. The adjacent
chapel of Saint Zeno, also 9th century, displays especially
fine mosaics, including one of what is surely a female bishop.
The architectural setting is a good example of ancient Rome
recycled into Christian use.

CHARLES WITKE
Classicist, University of Michigan

The construction of the church itself is an artistic "collage"
of even older Roman architectural remnants. The visitor is
truly in the presence of late antiquity. It is also still a place
of genuine modern religious devotion (because of the collection of relics) which many will find of interest.

JAMES M. LATTIS
Historian of Astronomy, University of Wisconsin–Madison

Built by Pascal I, one of the great medieval papal patrons, Santa Prassede is based on the early Christian model of Old St. Peter's and its apse mosaic "copies" the 6th-century apse of Santi Cosma and Damiano or a similar now-destroyed model. The ensemble shows the early Christian source and its medieval transformations. Rome's great monument from the age of Charlemagne.

ROBERT P. BERGMAN (1945–1999)
Director, Cleveland Museum of Art (1993–1999)

Chapel of St. Zeno

In this small and not very high space, one is surrounded by the mosaic surface—mostly gold—and the figures of apostles, saints, angels, Christ, etc. The mosaic pieces are quite large and transitions abrupt, giving an effect often called "expressionistic" with some analogies to such effects in the work of early 20th-century German painters and printmakers. It is all of a piece so while within this chapel one really is in a bit of the world of the 9th century. The mosaic in the apse of the main church is of Saints Peter and Paul presenting the two local female saints, Prassede and Pudenziana, to Christ. In doing so, each has an encouraging hand on the shoulder of the lady being presented.

JAMES FOWLE
Art historian (retired), Rhode Island School of Design

ALSO RECOMMENDED BY
AL BLAUSTEIN, WALTER HOOD, JOHN KENFIELD, EUGENE (GENE) MATTHEWS

2.9 ## Basilica of Santa Maria Maggiore
Piazza di Santa Maria Maggiore

The splendid mosaics in the nave from the 5th century are one of the finest and latest examples of Roman art.

RICHARD FRANK
Classicist, historian, University of California–Irvine

Cappella Sforza
Giacomo Della Porta, from design by Michelangelo

I consider the chapel a sculpture of space. The volume expands laterally and simultaneously is strapped tightly together. It isn't completely realized as Michelangelo intended, but it can be considered the harbinger of all the virtuoso "sculpted" interiors by Bernini, Borromini, and subsequent Italians and southern Germans.
D. B. MIDDLETON
Architect

ALSO RECOMMENDED BY
FRANCES BLANK, PAMELA STARR

RECOMMENDED READING 1

2.10   ## Santa Pudenziana

4th century
via Urbana 160

Like so many buildings in Rome, this exquisite little church is set well below the present street level. One can see, by observing the early columns embedded in later arches, how an early Christian basilica was later altered to a more Baroque form. The apse mosaic is magnificent, a demonstration of purely classical pictorial methods of shading, perspective, and realistic use of color, all applied to Christian subject material.
SUSAN WOOD
Art historian, Oakland University

2.11   ## Teatro dell'Opera

via Firenze 72, ☎ 06 48 17 003, 06 48 81 755

Training ground for many stars. Get the cheapest seats, the wooden benches way up referred to as "the sparrows' roost." Sit next to weeping older men in well-worn suits, hats in their laps, knees together, in from the countryside, to participate in the spectacle. It's the same spectacle that is taking place outside in the rest of the city: sex, death, money, gossip, intrigue, scheming, and resolve. It makes Italy make sense. Bring the libretto of whatever opera you are seeing.
ROSS ANDERSON
Architect

ALSO RECOMMENDED BY
PAUL CLOGAN, WALTER HOOD

2.12 Museo Nazionale Romano in Palazzo Massimo alle Terme

Largo di Villa Peretti, opposite the Baths of
Diocletian

Frescoes of Livia's Garden Room from the Villa di Livia at Prima Porta

1st century BC

The most beautiful painting and painted room I've ever
seen. A forerunner of Rousseau, Matisse, and Gauguin.
MELISSA MEYER
Artist

These paintings are sublime. One can sense what a rich
Roman's cool, underground summer dining room was like.
Every plant, tree, and shrub bears fruit or flowers. Layers
of foliage and patterns pile up surrounding the viewer in
an atmosphere ripe and fragrant. There are said to be sixty-
nine identifiable kinds of birds and twenty-four kinds of
tree and shrub. I know of no other place in Rome where one
can better experience the private luxury that Prima Porta
represented.
DENNIS CONGDON
Artist, Rhode Island School of Design

For a visitor who has seen the more famous Augustan monuments of Rome, this series of frescoes reveals how Augustus
and Livia sought to express their power in the detailing of a
simple yet luxuriant garden scene, with vigorous young trees
within the garden fence and an abundance of fruit and flow-
ering plants beyond, all displayed at their peak as if all seasons
were compressed into a single timeless place.
KATHRYN GLEASON
*Landscape archaeologist, Cornell University, co-principal
investigator of the American Academy in Rome Excavation at
Horace's Villa, Licenza*

The fresco ensemble fascinates me by its simultaneous marginality to the official, "monumental" Rome and its central role in the private life of wealthy and powerful Romans.

It is a real pleasure to imagine the emperor and his wife, Livia, sharing this suburban retreat and, especially, its subterranean garden room. Theirs seems to have been one of the real love stories of ancient Rome: it is hard to see what considerations beyond passion might have led Augustus to steal the young and pregnant Livia from her husband and take her and her three-year-old son to his own house. Livia's reputation amongst later historians for poisonous tendencies and stepmotherly trickery is nicely balanced, I think, by the tale of joyous omens, which gave its name to the suburban property on their wedding day.

This subterranean room (20' x 30') illustrates the Roman architect's (and patron's) joy in playing with limits. Completely unwindowed and sunk into the ground, the room pretended to open into a sunny garden filled with birds, plants, and fountains. The skylike background is a light, daytime blue. The upper register seems to represent the entrance of a grotto, from which, perhaps, the viewer spies the garden. The scene has a splendid sense of depth, created by variations in detail work on the painted trees and flowers.

On the most blisteringly hot day, it offered the illusion of a cool springtime garden retreat. Scholars see it as possibly the earliest example (approximately 30–20 BC) of a pictorial type which continued to be popular throughout the Imperial period. Livia and Augustus, no surprise, were on the cutting edge of architectural fashion, though not—typical of Augustus—in a manner which called public attention to itself. This kind of luxury could be shared with family and friends without injury to Augustus' reputation for "Republican" simplicity in matters of domestic space.

The gift shop at Palazzo Massimo is exquisite; bring lots of money or "plastic."

LINDA W. RUTLAND GILLISON
Classicist, University of Montana

ALSO RECOMMENDED BY
ROBERT HAMILTON, MARTIE HOLMER, DAVID KONSTAN, EUGENE (GENE) E. MATTHEWS, ANN MCCOY, VIRGINIA

Paquette, William O. Smith, Anne Weis

RECOMMENDED READING 60, 64

Frescoes from the Villa Farnesina

A building less surely attributed, found at the Villa Farnesina in Trastevere during work on the Tiber embankment between 1879 and 1885, housed the other set of frescoes displayed next to Livia's gardenlike walls in Palazzo Massimo. When the Villa della Farnesina, not to be confused with the Renaissance Farnesina, on which property it was discovered, came to light, it was identified with the *horti Clodiae*, the park owned, between 65 and 45 BC at least, by a certain Roman matron named Clodia. On the occasion of a legal run-in with her in 56 BC, the wordmaster Cicero had noted her choice of river-bank site for her park as a vantage from which she could observe Rome's youth as they swam and thus choose her next young attachment. However inventive Cicero (and perhaps his younger contemporary Catullus) may have been in regard to her character, the enticing image of the wealthy, dissolute Roman noblewoman easing her ennui in the riverside park lodged itself in many a scholarly male brain, and the Villa Farnesina immediately "became" the *horti Clodiae*. Longer study dated the building and its decoration decades post-Clodia, at approximately 20 BC. Presently another intriguing and better-founded theory associates it with Julia, daughter of Augustus, and her much older husband Agrippa, the Princeps' closest confidant.

Make time for the rest of the splendid museum. It's a rich field, though, and a careful visit would consume days.
Linda W. Rutland Gillison
Classicist, University of Montana

ALSO RECOMMENDED BY
Gregory S. Bucher

2.13 Baths of Diocletian

Emperors Diocletian and Maximian, 298–306 AD
Piazza della Repubblica 12

The largest and most impressive of all the bath complexes

in Rome itself, occupying about twenty-seven acres of land, the Baths of Diocletian are said to have accommodated about 3,000 bathers, almost twice as many people as served by the Baths of Caracalla.

Today, the remains of the cold room (*frigidarium*) alone contain the entire church of Santa Maria degli Angeli (designed by Michelangelo in 1561). Part of the Museo Nazionale Romano (Terme Museum) was built into the rooms on the eastern side of the building; an outdoor display of classical sculpture occupies what was once an open-air exercise room (*palaestra*).

The present street plan of the Piazza dell'Esedra (Piazza della Repubblica) follows the shape of the original structure. At the top of the via Nazionale, let your eyes sweep in both directions along the curved façades and porticos of the Risorgimento buildings which front the piazza. That semi-circle follows the outer limits of the Baths' curved *exedra*. You enter the present church of Santa Maria degli Angeli through a door in a small, curved apse, the only preserved part of the rectangular hot room (*caldarium*). The warm room (*tepidarium*), its dome filled with *trompe l'oeil* coffers, leads into the main hall of the church, which Michelangelo designed to fill the space of the former *frigidarium* with its basilicalike vaulting, clerestory windows (some now filled with paintings), and enormous columns retaining the grandiose feeling of the original structure. As you experience the room's overwhelming proportions, remember that it is only the central part of the original structure. In 1749, the architect Vanvitelli added the choir and apse which extend north into the central area of the original swimming pool.

What you cannot see are the changing rooms with the niches for lockers where clothes of the bathers would have been guarded by slaves. Nor can you see the rooms where those who came for exercise were rubbed down with oil before going into the *palaestra* to work out with weights, play catch, wrestle, box, or fence. Not visible, either, are the Greek and Latin libraries (Diocletian probably kept the precious volumes from Trajan's Ulpian Library here); we can only imagine the shops for food and drink. There also would have been gardens and an outdoor running track—the

Baths were not just for bathing, they were social centers where Romans spent entire afternoons.
NORMA GOLDMAN
Classicist, Wayne State University

RECOMMENDED READING 114

2.14 Santa Maria degli Angeli

Michelangelo, 1563–1566; Vanvitelli, 1749
Piazza della Repubblica

Santa Maria degli Angeli is one church a person might not visit unless prompted. The contrast between the "pile of bricks" look at entry and the magnificent interior volumes and Roman bath history makes it a "must see."
CRAIG H. WALTON
Architect

2.15 Museo Nazionale Romano in Museo delle Terme

via Enrico Nicola 79, ☎ 06 48 82 364

Pugilist
Apollonius, 1st century BC

Not only a beautiful sculpture but a wonderful opportunity to meet an actual "gladiator"—a great romantic experience for me.
ALDO CASANOVA
Sculptor, Scripps College

Magnificent example of ancient bronze work, displayed in a lovely interior located in part of the ancient bath structure. Accessible at close range.
HELEN NAGY
Art historian, University of Puget Sound, Washington

It is expressionistic and powerful. Look for incising and the dynamic of the head being turned an impossible ninety-degree angle from the chest.
SIMON DINNERSTEIN
Artist, New School for Social Research/Parsons School of Design

Niobid

School of Kresilas, 5th century BC

In contrast with the Pugilist, this is a dazzling, superbly beautiful and *echt*-classical depiction of woman.

SIMON DINNERSTEIN
Artist

3

4

2

N

THE QUIRINALE

1. Galleria Colonna
✕ 2. Ristorante Abruzzi ai SS. Apostoli
3. Casino dell'Aurora Pallavicini
4. Sant'Andrea al Quirinale
5. San Carlo alle Quattro Fontane ("San Carlino")
6. Santa Maria della Concezione ("I Cappuccini")
7. Galleria Nazionale d'Arte Antica in Palazzo Barberini
8. Collegio di Propaganda Fide
✕ 9. Al Moro
✕ 10. Gelateria San Crispino
11. Santa Maria della Vittoria

3.1 Galleria Colonna

Palazzo Colonna
via della Pilotta 17, ☎ 06 67 94 362
open Saturday only 9:00 a.m.–1:00 p.m.

Venus and Cupid and a Satyr
Bronzino, 1555

This painting, tight in composition, slightly "kinky" in its
presentation, is not of the general stock found in U.S.
museums. The delicate colors are hard to capture in repro-
duction...a unique experience and new images that surprise.
CHARLES K. WILLIAMS II
*Archaeologist, emeritus director of the Corinth excavation,
American School of Classical Studies, Athens*

3.2 Ristorante Abruzzi ai SS. Apostoli

via del Vaccaro 1, ☎ 06 67 93 897

Best pasta carbonara *bar none* in Rome. (I attempted to try
them all.) Is the recipe the same twenty years later? If so,
order *primo* and *secondo*.
CRAIG WALTON

3.3 Casino dell'Aurora Pallavicini

Giovanni Vesanzio, 1603
Palazzo Pallavicini Rospigliosi
via XXVI Maggio 43

The palace itself is always closed (the Princess Pallavicini is
ninety-one and wheelchair-bound) but the casino and garden are opened to the public on the first day of each month.

On the appropriate day, ring at the gate to the walled
garden for entry into this intimate green space, complete
with a mossy grotto, and, best of all, the delicate pink "casino."
The casino and palace were designed by Giovanni Vesanzio
in 1603, who also did the Villa Borghese for the same patron,
the Cardinal Scipione Borghese. Marvelous relief panels
from ancient sarcophagus sides and other classical bas-reliefs
adorn the casino's façade. Inside is Guido Reni's famous
ceiling fresco *Aurora Leading the Chariot of Apollo* (1613),

which has just been cleaned. The casino has one large state room and two side rooms, one of which has the cartoon for the Reni fresco.

In addition, as it is one of the highest points in the city, the Casino has perhaps the best sunset view in Rome, looking across toward the Vatican residence. The overall experience is heavenly, especially at dusk when white-gloved servants from the palazzo are serving *spumante* and gorgeous hors d'oeuvres.

Wendy Moonan
Journalist

3.4 Sant'Andrea al Quirinale

Bernini, 1670
via del Quirinale 29

One of Bernini's most perfect works in architecture. His son, Domenico, tells us that in old age his father liked to come to the church and enjoy it; so, too, should we. Designed around a simple oval plan, with the short axis leading to the high altar, every step, from the street through the portico to the exterior, has been choreographed by the architect. The martyrdom of Saint Andrew is depicted by Borgognone on the high altar with God the Father in the small dome above. Saint Andrew, in stucco, ascends atrium level, the heavenly host awaits him at the lantern base, and the Holy Dove appears in the lantern ceiling. Spectacular!

Malcolm Campbell
Art historian, University of Pennsylvania

This small oval church on the Quirinal Hill has such a beautiful feeling of ecstatic spirituality. One is filled with quietude and joy as light pours in from above illuminating the choir of scintillating child angels. The structure is humanly sized and creates a very personal and comforting awareness of God's presence within all of us.

Janis Bell
Holistic educator, spiritual healer, art historian

ALSO RECOMMENDED BY
Barbara Goldsmith, Wendy Evans Joseph

Shrine room of Saint Stanislas
Sculpture by Pierre LeGros, 17th century

Accessed from Sant'Andrea, via a back door from within the church, one enters the palazzo next door, ascends a flight of stairs, enters an apartment, and in the bedroom is LeGros's amazing deathbed memorial to the Polish Saint Stanislas Kostka, who is said to have traveled all the way to Rome on his knees. The marble is exquisitely handled, not only in the saint's face and figure, but also his several coverlets, brilliantly colored, flying off in every direction. A sight to behold and, considering what it must have cost, as good a reason as any for the Protestant Reformation.

BARRY LEWIS
Architectural historian

The image of Stanislas, on a marble bed, is not the general conceptual presentation for a saint, but it seems the essence of the period and the period's religious attitudes—a unique statement.

CHARLES K. WILLIAMS II
Archaeologist, emeritus director of the Corinth excavation, American School of Classical Studies, Athens

3.5 San Carlo alle Quattro Fontane ("San Carlino")
Borromini, 1665–1668
via del Quirinale 23

One of the most subtle and original buildings of the Roman Baroque, and a source of endless pleasure for anyone who enjoys the play of space, light, and texture in architecture. A masterpiece by one of Italy's most unusual designers and a work so skillfully integrated into a given piece of Rome's monumental townscape.

JOHN WILTON-ELY
Art historian, Fellow of the Society of Antiquaries, London, and Royal Society of Arts

This is a complete work of sculpture masquerading as a building. The contrapuntal rhythm of its curves and the complete inversion of interior and exterior space is breathtaking.

This building shows that the distinctions among painting, sculpture, and architecture disappear in the work of a great artist.

WALTER CHATHAM
Architect

Intimacy and grandeur in one tiny building; all of Borromini's pent-up genius explodes here. Meanwhile, archrival Bernini was blithely dispersing his prodigious talent on multiple sites all around Quattro Fontane (Sant'Andrea al Quirinale, Palazzo Barberini, Fountain of Triton in Piazza Barberini, etc.).

DAVID PISCUSKAS
Architect

After seeing the dome and crossing piers of St. Peter's, keep in mind the size of the plan of one of its piers—and realize, as Paolo Portoghesi pointed out, that the entire plan of San Carlino could fit within that space. A comparison of San Carlino's own piers, arches, oval dome, and lantern should be maintained with the interior of St. Peter's. The smaller church's dependence on that model will help the viewer to decipher its clear structure and rational format despite the profusion of its resplendent and brilliant decoration and embellishment.

THOMAS GORDON SMITH
Architect, University of Notre Dame

ALSO RECOMMENDED BY
JOSEPH CONNORS, ELFRIEDE AND GEORG KNAUER,
SUSAN MOLESKY

RECOMMENDED READING 20, 92, 112

3.6 Santa Maria della Concezione ("I Cappuccini")

1626
via Veneto 27

Cimitero dei Cappuccini

Is it possible to make human bones into things of beauty? (And don't miss the celebrated painting by Guido Reni,

Saint Michael and the Devil, on the altar of the first chapel of the right nave.)
WILLIAM E. WALLACE
Art historian, author, Washington University

3.7 Galleria Nazionale d'Arte Antica at Palazzo Barberini

Carlo Maderno, Bernini, and Borromini, 1625–1633
via delle Quattro Fontane 13, ☎ 06 48 14 591

Every first-class architect in 17th-century Rome worked here and the visitor can have fun looking for traces of each one's hand and style. The fascinating façade was based on Raphael's design for the Farnesina and other Renaissance sources. Carlo Maderno was the original architect. Square staircase = Bernini; circular = Borromini. Then there is the spectacular vault fresco by Pietro da Cortona. The complex is really a double palace as enlarged in the 17th century. It was originally commissioned in 1625 by Pope Urban VIII Barberini, the reigning pope. It houses a magnificent art collection, the Galleria Nazionale d'Arte Antica.
MALCOLM CAMPBELL
Art historian, University of Pennsylvania

RECOMMENDED READING 43, 107

Allegory of Divine Providence
Pietro da Cortona, 1632–1639

One of the greatest decorative ceilings of the Baroque.
JAMES S. ACKERMAN
Art historian, Harvard University

The frescoed ceiling is notable for its scale, complexity, setting, movement.
FRANC PALAIA
Painter, photographer, muralist, curator

ALSO RECOMMENDED BY
THOMAS GORDON SMITH

RECOMMENDED READING 87

Madonna and Child with the Young Saint John
Domenico Beccafumi, 1525–1535

The color palette and hallucinatory light in this painting are staggering. The composition of the Madonna and Child seems transformed by a visionary light, and the icy pinks, golds, and greens radiate. Fingers and limbs are elongated; drapery is faceted, edgy, and prismatic. Clearly Beccafumi was inspired by his Roman sojourns and his contact with Mannerist painters like Rosso Fiorentino or even Pontormo. However, the picture has a Gothicizing aura to it which must surely come from his Sienese origins. It is a riveting but a somewhat rarified painting. It is especially interesting to those who are seduced by both artifice and Mannerism. The Christ Child seems literally to be emerging from the Virgin's stomach. As many of the paintings of this period, it is erotic in content. I adore the picture.
JUDITH DIMAIO
Architect, Yale University

3.8   ### Collegio di Propaganda Fide

Borromini, 1622
via Due Macelli

Two of the greatest architectural competitors of the 17th century, Bernini, the courtier, and Borromini, the outsider, can best be seen side by side in two places. Beginning in the Piazza di Spagna, the Palace of the Propaganda Fide has a restrained façade on the northern side by Bernini, and then a group of unorthodox doors and windows by Borromini on the via di Propaganda façade. On that same side, if you enter the courtyard (where generally tourists aren't allowed) a tip to the *portiere* will usually get you into Borromini's Chapel of the Re Magi. Here is a sparse Baroque space with intricate geometry. The doorman told me once that Borromini had *"modernizzato il barocco."*

Just a few steps away in via Capo le Case is the church of Sant'Andrea delle Fratte, where the two masters can be seen again. This time, a bell tower by Borromini, which must have been radical when built in flat Roman bricks with all of its convex and concave turns, and, inside the church, two angels carved by Bernini himself that are prototypes for those on the Ponte Sant'Angelo.

VINCENT BUONANNO
Book collector

RECOMMENDED READING 25

3.9   **Al Moro**

vicolo delle Bollette 13, ☎ 06 67 83 495

Go to Al Moro during lunchtime in the fall. The place is bustling with Romans doing business and politics, and the table full of fresh porcini and oviolo mushrooms that greets you upon entering sets the stage for a perfect lunch. I'd eat roast mushrooms and potatoes for my *secondo* preceded by *maccheroni al Moro*—the house version of the best carbonara you're liable to taste anywhere.

DANNY MEYER

The only time I saw Alberto Moravia was at Al Moro. It's not outlandishly expensive and gives you a special flavor of the elegance and wit of dining out in Rome.

DAVID ST. JOHN

ROME'S LATIN INSCRIPTIONS

NE GLORIARI LIBEAT ALIENIS BONIS (*"Do not take pleasure in boasting of the goods of another."*)

A quotation from the fable of Phaedrus about the jackdaw who dresses himself in the finery of a peacock. The Latin is of indeterminate date and appears in an inscription over the door of a *pizza al taglio*, or take-out pizzeria, in via delle Muratte, a few steps from the Trevi Fountain.

PAUL PASCAL
Classicist, University of Washington

3.10 Gelateria San Crispino

Take via del Lavatore to the right of the Trevi
Fountain, then turn left on via della Panetteria.

The best gelato in Rome is found at the rather new, pristine
San Crispino around the corner from the Trevi Fountain.
The Sicilian orange sorbetto and aged armagnac ice cream
will make you return to the Fountain and toss the coins again.
KENNETH FRAZELLE

Intense flavors and completely natural ingredients.
ARTHUR LEVERING

3.11 Santa Maria della Vittoria

via XX Settembre 17

Ecstasy of Saint Theresa
Bernini, 1645–1652
Cornaro Chapel

This is a beautiful example of Bernini's ability to combine
space, light, color, architecture, and sculpture into an
experience that is theatrical and sensuous yet spiritual and
visionary. Be sure to go in the afternoon to get the full
effect of Bernini's incorporation of outside light into the
composition. Walk down the nave of the church and as you
approach the last chapel on the left you first see the Cornaro
cardinals and as you reach the entrance to the chapel you
turn and see what they are watching with such excitement.
Wonderfully natural sculptures of the cardinals in what
appear to be theater boxes flank the stage where Saint
Theresa is swooning in rapture, suspended on a stucco
cloud. An angel who has descended with the light (gilded
rays lit by a hidden stained-glass window admitting exterior
light) is piercing her heart with his arrow.
JEAN WEISZ
Art historian, University of California–Los Angeles

Most dazzling of all Bernini's *concetti*, this theatrical, indeed
operatic opus—complete with flanking sculptural groups look-

ing on from box seats—is the epitome of Baroque flamboyance
but also surprisingly moving in its embodiment of spiritual
abandon. Of all commentaries on its frank exposure of the
sexual nature of religious devotion, my favorite is the observation of the President de Brosses, who wrote, *"Si c'est ici
l'amour divin, je le connais"* (If this is divine love, I know it).
MARTIN FILLER
Architecture critic and curator

Best one-stop opportunity to capture the full sense of the
Baroque style. Created in the left transept of the church
by Bernini for Cardinal Frederico Cornaro, this is Baroque
style as "theater" in the best sense. Deceased members of
the Cornaro family and the Cardinal debate theological
issues from side galleries while the ecstatic saint "appears"
before the viewer as if cloud-borne, bathed in a spiritual
light, and receiving the stigmata from a heaven-sent angel.
The illusionism of the chapel encompasses a range of inter-
related spheres: the heaven of the frescoed vault (fresco by
Aggatini, based on a Bernini sketch), the visionary world of
Saint Theresa, and the material world (ours and the Cornaro
skeletons' in the inlaid marble floor of the chapel).
MALCOLM CAMPBELL
Art historian, University of Pennsylvania

ALSO RECOMMENDED BY
MARK ADAMS, MARY BETTS ANDERSON, GIANNE HARPER,
J. RICHARD JUDSON, ELFRIEDE AND GEORG KNAUER,
ROBERT LIVESEY, GERDA S. PANOFSKY, REBECCA WEST

RECOMMENDED READING 4, 52, 62, 63, 113

Sant'Agnese fuori le Mura

4th century, rebuilt 7th century
via Nomentana 349 (not shown on map)

Visit the church, its grounds, and the smaller church of
Santa Costanza and the bocce courts where you can watch
experts at this old Italian bowling game. In the same small
delightful park with Santa Costanza, Sant'Agnese is one of

Borromini's Rome

Spend a day with Francesco Borromini, the 17th-century architect who lost many clients and commissions to his archrival Bernini, but who nevertheless produced some of the best and most imaginative Baroque buildings in Rome.

San Carlo alle Quattro Fontane (known affectionately as San Carlino). Façade completed in 1668. The subtle and complex geometry of this small eight-sided space is dazzling.

Sant'Ivo. Completed in 1660. Borromini's ingenuous hexagonal plan creates bays that evolve from concave to straight-sided to convex, sweeping up to a dramatic spiral lantern. The art historian Rudolf Wittkower delighted in Sant'Ivo: "Geometric succinctness and inexhaustible imagination, technical skill and religious symbolism, have rarely found such a reconciliation."

Palazzo Spada. In 1652, Borromini created a *trompe l'oeil* which appears to be a long colonnade leading to a heroic statue, but is in fact a clever trick of illusion.

Sant'Agnese in Agone. The elegantly concave 1650s façade is nearly all Borromini's design (but, alas, a committee of architects also became involved).

Collegio di Propaganda Fide. The whole façade has been called a study "in compression and dilation." Inside the building is Borromini's exquisite Chapel of the Re Magi.

JOHN JAY STONEHILL, ARCHITECT
AND JUDITH STONEHILL

the few examples of a Greek gallery-aisled basilica in Rome.
JOHN KENFIELD
Archaeologist and art historian, Rutgers University

What a combination: Honorius' 7th-century church, restored
more than once and "evolved" as Roman churches do, provides a remarkably quiet and detached atmosphere in which
to view the lovely apse mosaic of Sant'Agnese. In back, the
4th-century circular church of Santa Costanza has, in the
vault of its circular ambulatory, absolutely beautiful mosaics
as "classical" and "early" as any Christian mosaics in Rome.
The patterns are on a white ground; some are geometrical,
others are of vines with grape-gathering cupids, scattered
branches, fruits, and ceramic pots of a type that you can still
buy in Rome. The grounds are on several levels with oleander-
lined paths. Don't miss the old (and young) men at the bocce
courts!
JAMES FOWLE
Art historian, Rhode Island School of Design

RECOMMENDED READING 50

Santa Costanza

4th century
behind Sant'Agnese fuori le Mura
(not shown on map)

This quiet, little-visited church is an astonishing survivor
of the cusp between the late Roman and early Christian
worlds. The glorious mosaic barrel vaults of the ambulatory
that surrounds the circular sanctuary justify a visit in themselves, and their iconography of winemaking—at once
sensuously pagan and symbolic of the Eucharist—provides
the perfect emblem of that transitional era. Built by the
emperor Constantine's elder daughter Constantia as a mausoleum for herself and her sister Helena, it is additionally
significant as a link to the Imperial convert.
MARTIN FILLER
Architecture critic and curator

A development of the mausoleum's circular form for the emperor Constantine — similar to the Pantheon, but with its dome at about half the Pantheon's in size, set on a double row of twelve columns. The building is an important archetype for several reasons, including its use of exquisite mosaics, which spread through the growing Christian world to ecclesiastical buildings in Ravenna and Constantinople, as well as its survival for 1200 years, which made it an important archetype of Roman architecture for the Renaissance. It eventually influenced the Baroque manifestations of elliptical domes floating above the columnar structures and walls in the work of Borromini (e.g., San Carlo alle Quattro Fontane) and Bernini (e.g., Sant'Andrea al Quirinale).

ROBERT EVANS
Architect

Santa Costanza's domed rotunda conforms to the design of Imperial mausolea, and most probably was built for Constantia, who died in 354 and was buried in or near the cemetery church commemorating the catacomb and grave of Saint Agnes. Recent archaeological discoveries support a date in the late 4th or early 5th century for the mausoleum, but this would mean that it was completed long after her death. The porphyry sarcophagus (a plaster copy exists in place of the original, which was moved to the Vatican Museum), carved with vintage scenes related to the mosaics, attests that this was her mausoleum. The rich polychrome mosaics are the earliest and most admired of the early Christian mosaics of Rome. Set against white backgrounds, they lighten the darker ambulatory, and the designs are executed in identical pairs of geometric designs, scattered foliage, Dionysian objects, and grape harvest scenes set in an overhead arbor with busts of the deceased. These are the same compositions found underfoot in private houses of the 3rd and 4th centuries.

A few decades later, a church was dedicated to Saint Stephen protomartyr on the Celian Hill (Santo Stefano Rotondo, see page 210). Built by Pope Simplicius (468–483), the plan of three concentric rings, one outer and two inner, suggests that the building functioned as a

martyrium sheltering the relics of Saint Stephen. Like that of
Santa Costanza, this plan is shaped by outer and inner rings
around a cylindrical core; similarly, a colonnade articulates
the inner circle, which is lit by windows at the base of the
dome. At Santo Stefano there are four chapels laid crosswise which provide axial counterpoints to the circular plan.
Faced with rich marble revetments now lost, Santo Stefano
is a bit less celebrative than Santa Costanza; the latter is
after all the favored spot for nuptials in Rome.

In both buildings we experience a masterful choreography
of space, light, and materials, of interpenetrating spaces
and surprising alternations. Go there to think about architecture, about innovation, about the circle and the square.

CHRISTINE KONDOLEON
Curator of Greek and Roman Art, Worcester Art Museum

A beguiling example of the confusions of time and motive
experienced in any given place in Rome. With the eyes of
someone who has just emerged into the sun from the
Catacombs of Sant'Agnese—that is how I first saw the Church
of Santa Costanza, and in my memory continue to see it.
Minutes before, sepulchered in a maze of narrow tunnels
and surrounded by the crude drawings of doves, crosses,
and fish that appeared out of darkness (even as they must
have done when the beleaguered Christians turned their
lamps and tapers upon them), I had been moved by the ter-
ror and faith those people must have known there under the
earth. Once back in the light, I carried the impression of the
forms they left behind to the adjacent church-mausoleum
built a century later by the daughter of Constantine, the all-
powerful first Roman-Christian emperor.

Though Constantia's church is lucidly, touchingly simple
by Roman standards, it was built as a memorial to herself by
the daughter of a proud, even megalomanical emperor whose
ambitions were the very antithesis of what inspired the people who had prayed for eternal life below. Indeed, the beauty
of the church's circular design and of its mosaic decoration—
the vintage scenes, grapes, fruits, peacocks, birds, animals,
and natural forms of every kind that appear on the vaulted
ceiling—are probably not the outgrowth of Christian iconog-

raphy at all. As unforgettable as the elegant building is, its structure and decoration most likely follow long-established pagan conventions only minimally influenced by the Christians.

JANET SULLIVAN
Writer, Rhode Island School of Design

ALSO RECOMMENDED BY
URSULA HEIBGES, WALTER HOOD, J. RICHARD JUDSON, LYNN KEARNEY, MARJORIE KREILICK

RECOMMENDED READING 60, 81, 93

ROME'S LATIN INSCRIPTIONS

INNOCENTIUS DECIMUS PONTIFEX MAXIMUS
NILOTICIS AENIGMATIBUS EXARATUM LAPIDEM
AMNIBUS SUBTERLABENTIBUS IMPOSUIT UT SALUBREM
SPATIANTIBUS AMOENITATEM, SITIENTIBUS POTUM,
MEDITANTIBUS ESCAM MAGNIFICE LARGIRETUR
("Pope Innocent X erected this stone, engraved with the riddles of the Nile, over flowing fountains, in order to lavish healthful pleasure on promenaders, drink on the thirsty, and food for thought on the thinkers.")

One of four 17th-century inscriptions at the base of the obelisk in Piazza Navona. The other three inscriptions are equally pompous.

PAUL PASCAL
Professor emeritus of classics, University of Washington

PIAZZA DI SPAGNA,
VILLA BORGHESE
AND
PIAZZA DEL POPOLO

4

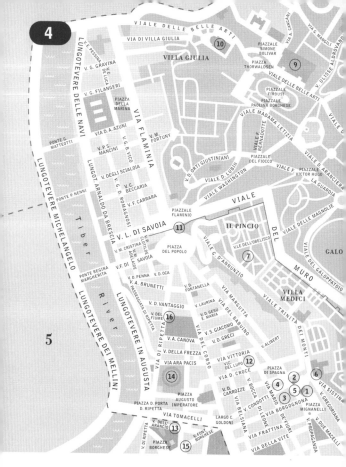

4

PIAZZALE SIMONE BOLIVAR
PIAZZALE THORWALDSEN
PIAZZALE FIRDUSI
PIAZZALE PAOLINA BORGHESE
PIAZZALE DEL FIOCCO
PIAZZALE VICTOR HUGO
LA GUARDIA

VIALE DELLE BELLE ARTI
VIA DI VILLA GIULIA
VILLA GIULIA
VIALE DELLE BELLE ARTI
VIALE MADAMA LETIZIA
VIALE BERNADOTTE
VIALE D. ARANCIERA
VIA C. CANONICA
VIA G. MANGILI
VIA ULISSE ALDROVANDI

LUNGOTEVERE DELLE NAVI
V.LE PESSINA
V.G. DE LUCA
V.G. GRAVINA
V.G. FILANGERI
PIAZZA DELLA MARINA
VIA D.A. AZUNI
VIA FLAMINIA
V.M. FORTUNY
V.D ORTI GIUSTINIANI
VIALE D. LUBIN
VIALE WASHINGTON
VIALE F. BERNADOTTE
VIALE F
PIAZZALE DEL FIOCCO

PONTE G. MATTEOTTI
PONTE P NENNI
V.P.S. MANCINI
V.G.B. VICO
V. DEGLI SCIALOJA
V.C. BECCARIA
V.G. ROMAGNOSI
V.F. CARRARA
PIAZZALE FLAMINIO
IL PINCIO
VIALE
DEL
MURO
VIALE DELLE MAGNOLIE
GALOP

LUNGOTEVERE MICHELANGELO
Tiber
PONTE REGINA MARGHERITA
LUNGOTEVERE ARNALDO DA BRESCIA
V.M. CRISTINA
V.L. DI SAVOIA
V.F. DI SAVOIA
PIAZZA DEL POPOLO
VIALE G. D'ANNUNZIO
V.LE DELL'OBELISCO
VIALE DEL GALOPPATOIO
GALO

River
LUNGOTEVERE DEI MELLINI
V.D. PENNA
V.D. OCA
V.A. BRUNETTI
V.D. FONTANELLA
VIA MARGUTTA
VILLA MEDICI
VIALE TRINITA DEI MONTI

5

LUNGOTEVERE IN AUGUSTA
V.D. VANTAGGIO
V.D. FIUME
V.A. CANOVA
V. DELLA FREZZA
VIA DI RIPETTA
VIA ARA PACIS
V. DEL CORSO
VIA LAURINA
V.D. GESU E. MARIA
VIA DEL BABUINO
V.S. GIACOMO
V.D. GRECI
V. ALIBERT
VIA VITTORIA
VIC. DEL LUPO
VIA D. CROCE
V.D. CARROZZE
V.D. BOCCA
VIA MARIO DE FIORI
DI LEONE
VIA CONDOTTI
VIA BORGOGNONA
PIAZZA DI SPAGNA
PIAZZA MIGNANELLI
VIA SISTINA
VIA GREGORIANA
V. DUE MACELLI
VIA PROPAGANDA

PIAZZA D. PORTA D. RIPETTA
PIAZZA AUGUSTO IMPERATORE
VIA TOMACELLI
LARGO C. GOLDONI
V. DELL'ARANCIO
V. DI RIPETTA
PIAZZA BORGHESE
V. FONTE BORGHESE
VIA BELSIANA
V. FRATTINA
VIA DELLA VITE

PIAZZA DI SPAGNA

1. Keats-Shelley Memorial
✕ 2. Babington's Tea Rooms
✕ 3. Ristorante Nino
✕ 4. Caffè Greco
5. Spanish Steps
✕ 6. Hotel Hassler Villa Medici

VILLA BORGHESE

✕ 7. Casina Valadier
8. Galleria Borghese
9. Galleria Nazionale
   d'Arte Moderna
10. Villa Giulia/Museo
    Nazionale Etrusco

GIARDINO
ZOOLOGICO

VIA G. CARISSIMI

VIA MERCADANTE V. N. PORPORA

VIALE DEL GIARDINO ZOOLOGICO

PIAZZALE DEL
GIARDINO
ZOOLOGICO

VIA G. B.
PERGOLESI

VIA P. RAIMONDI

VIA G. PAISIELLO

VIA
A. COELLI

VIALE DEL GIARDINO ZOOLOGICO

VIALE GIULIA

VIA PIETRO CANONICA

VIALE DELL'UCCELLIERA

PIAZZALE
DEI DAINI

11

VILLA
BORGHESE

PIAZZA
DI SIENA

VIALE DEI PUPAZZI

VIALE DELLE
DUE PIRAMIDI

PIAZZALE DEI
CAV. MARINI

(8)

PIAZZA DEL
MUSEO
BORGHESE

VIALE S. PAOLO DEL BRASILE

VIALE DELLA PINETA

VIALE GOETHE

VIALE DEL MUSEO BORGHESE

VIALE

VIA PINCIANA

ATOIO

PIAZZALE
BRASILE

TORTO

VIA DI PORTA PINCIANA

VIA F. CRISPI

3

PIAZZA DEL POPOLO
AND VICINITY

11. Santa Maria del Popolo

🏛 **12.** Vertecchi Stationery

✕ **13.** Trattoria da Settimio all'Arancio

14. Augustan Monumental Complex

🏛 **15.** Outdoor Print Market

✕ **16.** Buca di Ripetta

N

PIAZZA DI SPAGNA

Streets of Il Tridente

"Il Tridente" refers to the trident shaped by the three principal streets leading out of Piazza del Popolo: the via del
Corso, via del Babuino, and via di Ripetta, and includes the
cross streets and Piazza di Spagna itself. This is central
Rome's luxury shopping area and has great stores for all
sorts of things but, equally important, it has streets like via
della Croce with its small restaurants, cheese shops, deli-
catessens, coffee bars, pastry shops, and a small street market.
The Tridente shows how a downtown area can be both resi-
dential and commercial, touristy and indigenous. This is
the greatest achievement of Roman urbanism: things are
pleasant and the community works.
JAMES H. S. MCGREGOR
Professor of comparative literature, University of Georgia

ALSO RECOMMENDED BY
DAVID KONSTAN

4.1 Keats-Shelley Memorial
Piazza di Spagna 26

Its attractions include a portrait of former resident Axel
Munthe, the Swedish physician whose mystical experience
of Italy is recorded in *The Story of San Michele* and memori-
alized in his villa in Anacapri...itself worth a trip if one is
in the Naples area.
CATHERINE SPOTSWOOD GIBBES
Classical scholar, linguist, researcher, Hebrew College

This is where the poet John Keats lived during the last months
of his life (he was twenty-five years old when he died in
1821). The small old-fashioned museum located here houses
books, manuscripts, and portraits of the Romantic poets—
and seems a calm oasis next to the cacophony on the Spanish
Steps just outside the house. After visiting here, anyone
wanting to read "Ode to a Nightingale" can cross the river to

the charming and quirky English-language bookshop, the
Corner Bookstore, at via del Moro 48 in Trastevere.
John Jay Stonehill, *Architect*, and Judith Stonehill

4.2 Babington's Tea Rooms

Piazza di Spagna 23, ☎ 06 67 86 027,

This quintessentially English tearoom is an Anglo-Saxon
outpost at the corner of Mediterranean civilization. Sip tea
and eat crumpets while contemplating the fact that our concept of Rome is partly a product of Byron, et al., who chose
to see Rome as an abstract concept rather than a modern
metropolis.
Walter Chatham

It's small, nice, just for a rest.
Anton Rajer

NAMES OF ROME

The via del Babuino ("Street of the Baboon"), now known
for its upscale art galleries and shops, is named after an
ancient fountain with a carving that actually represents
Silenus, the grotesque drunken follower of Bacchus,
which was mistaken for an ape.
Paul Pascal
Classicist, University of Washington

4.3 Ristorante Nino

via Borgognona 11, ☎ 06 67 95 676

This Tuscan restaurant serves superb steaks, pastas, and
wines. Like all good Roman restaurants, they celebrate seasonal foods—it's an event when the first pappardelle in *sugo
di lepre* are served...the first *tartufi* of the season...the first
wild asparagus...the first *fragole dei boschi*...I could go on—

but I'm getting too homesick. The other reason this restaurant is special is the service. The waiters have all been here forever, and they treat you very well. Nino's has buzz at lunch—there's almost a New York bustle here—and I mean that only in the best sense.

PETER SCHWEITZER

NAMES OF ROME

Piazza di Spagna is so named because, since the 17th century, it has been the location of the Spanish Embassy to the Holy See. The adjoining via Condotti, for all its elegance, is named for something more prosaic: the aged conduits that feed water to the nearby Trevi Fountain.

PAUL PASCAL

Classicist, University of Washington

4.4   ## Caffè Greco

via Condotti 86, ☎ 06 67 82 554

A rather soigné interior, a souvenir of *Roma di una volta*, it's a pleasant place to have a drink and a rest from shopping in the via Condotti and surrounding streets.

BRUCE BOUCHER

To wander the streets of Rome is to travel through centuries of culture and life in a city where architecture and art have always been monumental. We feel ourselves quite insignificant within this grandeur. An hour spent in the Caffè Greco, on the other hand, is a very different experience because here we are transported to a world that we might feel connected to in earliest memories. This is a place that seems to be about nostalgia. The Caffè Greco is entirely unselfconsciously authentic, not a re-creation of anything, and that is why it remains so uniquely beautiful.

ALAN FELTUS

4.5 Spanish Steps

Francesco de Sanctis, 1726
Scalinata della Trinità dei Monti

A daring urbanistic device—and great window-shopping.
ANNE WEIS
Art historian, University of Pittsburgh

In spring, a riot of color as stunning for the tourists and
Romans who frequent it as for its intrinsic beauty.
BENJAMIN KOHL
Historian, Vassar College

ALSO RECOMMENDED BY
ROBERT CAMPBELL, MICHAEL CONFORTI, JEROME M.
COOPER, JOHN L. WONG

4.6 ROOF GARDEN OF HOTEL HASSLER VILLA MEDICI

Piazza Trinità dei Monti, ☎ 06 67 82 651

VIEW

*The most wonderful panorama of the city of Rome coupled with
magnificent food, ambience, and service.*
JUNE N. STUBBS AND JOHN C. STUBBS

ALSO RECOMMENDED BY
JOHN L. WONG

VILLA BORGHESE

4.7 Casina Valadier

Pincio Hill, ☎ 06 67 96 68, 67 92 083

My favorite thing to do is to walk up the Spanish Steps in
the evening, turn left and walk along the road to the outdoor
café at Casina Valadier in the Borghese Gardens, and then

sit and watch the sun go down over Rome.
WILLIAM TURPIN
Classicist, Swarthmore College

ALSO RECOMMENDED BY
GILBERT FRANKLIN

Miniature canal

Giardino del Lago, viale Pietro Canonica
(not shown on map)

Kids, and an occasional grownup, make paper yachts and
launch them from the head of a narrow, gravity-fed canal
spanned by some tiny bridges that winds through the beautiful park. Then the kids can prod their boats all the way to
the *lago* (lake) where they bob off out of range of the prod-
ding sticks and die a waterlogged death. A virtual-reality
reality that can take a long, blessedly child-engaged afternoon. A babysitting tour de force. The moms or nannies
(*tatas* to be exact) amble along, gossiping, knitting while
walking, knowing their charges are close by and engaged.
By the time it's over you're near the head of the Pincio overlook and it's time for *merenda* (a snack) and a Pulcinella
show. The Pincio overlooks the entire southeastern spread
of city rooftops, obelisks, and domes.
PIER CONSAGRA
Artist

4.8 Galleria Borghese

Piazzale Scipione Borghese 5, ☎ 06 85 48 577

Although much of Rome's beauty lies in its patina, the
sparkle of the newly reopened Galleria Borghese is quite
awesome. This is a rare time in history to see such a rich
environment where everything is as if new. The renovation
of the ground level also is a notable case study of an Italian
attitude toward the marriage of old and new.
BRUCE NORELIUS
Architect

This villa, built to house the extraordinary collection of
paintings and sculpture assembled by Cardinal Scipione
Borghese (1579–1633), nephew of Pope Paul V, is one of
the quintessential expressions of Roman civilization and
grandeur. In the galleries of the Villa Borghese, splendidly
redecorated in the late 18th century by Asprucci and
Unterberger, the visitor moves through chambers encrusted
with the rarest of materials—marble, bronze, alabaster—
and filled with works of art of a dazzling quality. Here is
Bernini's miraculous *Apollo and Daphne*, which captures
the nymph being transformed into a laurel tree, and a lithe
hermaphrodite from the 1st century AD; here is Caravaggio's
chillingly alluring *David with the Head of Goliath* and Fra
Bartolomeo's *The Adoration of the Christ Child*, one of the
most beautiful paintings in the world. But there is a very
special quality about the villa's first room. Beneath a dramatic fresco, *The Judgement of Paris*, Canova's glistening
white marble sculpture of Pauline Borghese, sister of
Napoleon, reclines upon a sumptuous couch, while opposite
Luigi Valadier's *Herm of Bacchus*, all luscious marble and
patinated copper, crowned by a wreath of gilded ivy leaves,
gazes across the splendid chamber. Within these four walls,
the noble saga of Rome, the Rome of history and myth, of
emperors and popes, of artists and cardinals, lives and
breathes.

David Garrard Lowe
Art historian, author

The creation of Cardinal Scipione Borghese, patron of Bernini,
this museum is truly a *Gesamtkunstwerk*: a personal collection of outstanding works of art in its original setting in the
park. Superbly restored recently.

Elfriede and Georg Knauer
*Classicist, University of Pennsylvania; Consulting scholar,
University Museum, University of Pennsylvania*

The likes of the Bernini statues in the collection cannot be
found elsewhere. Sculpture needs to be experienced in the
round. No virtual or photographic representation will do for
the twists and turns of these works (*Apollo and Daphne,*

Hades and Persephone, etc.).
CHARLES K. WILLIAMS II
Archaeologist, emeritus director of the Corinth excavation,
American School of Classical Studies, Athens

ALSO RECOMMENDED BY
GERALDINE ERMAN, RICHARD FRANK, CHARLES GWATHMEY,
ROSS KILPATRICK, STEVEN LOWENSTAM, CELIA SCHULTZ,
PAMELA STARR, THOMAS WATKINS

RECOMMENDED READING 13, 46, 113

Apollo and Daphne
Bernini, 1624

This 17th-century sculpture transforms the well-known
myth from Ovid's *Metamorphoses* into marble, and the
ancient Apollo Belvedere (in the Vatican) into Bernini's god
who runs after the nymph in vain. Another example of the
continuity of antiquity.
ANN THOMAS WILKINS
Classicist, Duquesne University

Rome is Bernini's town for the ages, and in his youth, when
he made this virtuosic work, he redefined what a sculptor
could be capable of. The marble becomes a flurry of light
and movement—a perfect expression of the pivotal moment
of a myth of transformation. Never surpassed for sheer
sculptural energy.
JEFFREY SCHIFF
Artist

The sculpture represents Daphne metamorphosing into a
tree to protect herself from Apollo's advances of love. You
see Daphne's fingertips and hair transforming into leaves,
and her ankles and feet becoming the trunk of a tree. You
actually think this is truly happening, and this sculpture
makes one realize the capability of stone to become imbued
with life. It is a sensuous, erotic, realistic, and beguiling
sculpture. Standing in this resplendent vaulted room in the
Borghese with this lacy white marble piece of "flesh" is a
divine experience. Art-historically, the sculpture represents

what has become known as Bernini's revolutionary concep-
tion; a transitory moment, the climax of an action; we the
spectators are drawn into this fictitious experience by a
"variety of devices."
JUDITH DIMAIO
Architect, Yale University

Dazzling bravura technique in a mythological scene sculpted
for a cardinal and the pope's nephew. Captures the spirit of
Ovid's *Metamorphoses* and the literary/cultural atmosphere
of early Baroque Rome.
DAVID G.WILKINS
Historian of art and architecture, University of Pittsburgh

ALSO RECOMMENDED BY
LIDIA MATTICCHIO BASTIANICH, WALTER CHATHAM, JUDY
DATER, ROBERT EVANS, MICHELE RENEE SALZMAN, CELIA
SCHULTZ, ROGER ULRICH, JOHN L. WONG

Rape of Proserpina
Bernini, 1621–1622

Experience the sense of the moment preserved. It does not
seem possible that the pressure of the splayed fingers upon
her thigh is sculpted from cold, hard marble. The gardens
of the villa and other sculptures are a delight which draw
you out of the busy urban present and into the past cultural
magnificence.
SLOAN RANKIN
Artist

ALSO RECOMMENDED BY
STEVEN LOWENSTAM

Aeneas and Anchises
Pietro Bernini and Gian Lorenzo Bernini, 1618–1619

Aeneas, Rome's founding forefather, carries elderly Anchises,
his father, while tiny son Ascanius follows along, just at his
father's heel. Anchises piously bears the *penates*—the house-
hold gods which must come along to bless any new city that
rises to replace the burned-out Troy.
　　This piece is marginal in the career of Gian Lorenzo

Bernini, as he worked on it as a teenager with his already famous sculptor father, Pietro. Gian Lorenzo's genius was patent early on, and he seems always to have been somewhat haughtily aware of it. The potential for competition between father and son is reflected in a purported exchange between the father and their papal patron. Urban VIII: "Watch out, Signor Bernini. This boy is going to outstrip you, and no doubt he will be more skillful than his teacher." Pietro in reply: "Your Eminence, remember that in such a game the loser is a winner."

Looking at this piece, I like to consider the father son relationship: the competition which probably was natural between Aeneas and his father Anchises, who, in fact, did not at first choose to leave Troy with his son and yet was, in the underworld, the only one who could assure his son of the destiny which awaited him; and the undying love which bound the two—and also the next generation represented by Ascanius— together as they fled Troy. In a sense, the very masculine figures of the group represent the masculinity of the Renaissance phenomenon. (Aeneas' wife Creusa has already been lost in the turmoil of the captured city and the past.) And, if the Renaissance is bearing classical antiquity, on its shoulders, out of the darkness of oblivion, is the little Ascanius the new trend—the Baroque spirit and verve and challenge at its peak—which the father Aeneas can't even fathom?

LINDA RUTLAND GILLISON
Classicist, University of Montana

Pauline Borghese
Canova, 1805–1808

This sculpture was meant to be seen by the light of one candle, but even better when the moon is out. During the summer you can ask to see it by moonlight (*chiar di luna*) and the guard will turn off the lights in the gallery. Sit there for twenty minutes to let your eyes adjust.

ROSS ANDERSON
Architect

ALSO RECOMMENDED BY
ANTON RAJER

Sacred and Profane Love
Titian, 1514

An early masterpiece painted as Titian sheds the influence
of his rival and mentor Giorgione. It is perhaps reading too
much into it that the very subject might be a metaphor for
that shedding, or a commemoration of his relationship to
his great Venetian elder, but I defy anyone not to make the
extrapolation, however far-flung, while standing in front of
this painting. Titian's allegory expresses a Hellenistic vision
interwoven with Christian significance, all bound up with
the formidable consequences of love.

Two Venuses, the divine and earthly, sit by a pool. The
earthly is sporting the latest Renaissance fashions, not to
mention a beautiful gold hasp, symbol of earthly vanity. The
divine is pure, and therefore naked, save for the famous
magic girdle.

Venus' son, Cupid, is busily immersing his hand into the
pool, perhaps cooling the stings of the bees whose honey he
has stolen and whose effects his mother, the celestial one,
points out are insignificant compared to the much deeper
wounds Cupid has inflicted. She is holding the lamp of
eternal love.

The rosebush and roses are sacred to Venus. (When she
accidentally pricked herself while helping the dying Adonis,
her blood turned a white flower into a red one, associating
her with Mary, thornless roses, prelapsarianism, and better
times.) Alexander the Great's famous white steed Bucephalus
is depicted on the frieze; Alexander himself is to the right
covering Darius after he was slain by his own men, an act of
great empathy, and very Christian.

This painting always reminds one of the immensely
seductive possibilities of the encounter between the ancients
and their Renaissance Christian apologists.

Pier Consagra
Artist

ALSO RECOMMENDED BY
Robert Campbell, Ross Kilpatrick

Boy with Basket of Fruit
Caravaggio, 1595

It's an amazing, unexpected painting and wonderful to see in the context of Rome.
SUSAN KLEINBERG
Artist

Borghese Faun
2nd-century Roman copy of a Greek original

The Borghese Faun or Satyr is a Roman copy of an original hollow-cast bronze by Lysippus or a member of his school, and is a subliminal example of Hellenistic baroque.
JOHN KENFIELD
Archaeologist and art historian, Rutgers University

4.9 Galleria Nazionale d'Arte Moderna
viale delle Belle Arti 131, ☎ 06 32 29 81

Many artists miss the paintings in the National Gallery of Modern Art, but I consider them highlights—two areas in particular. First, the "Scuola Romana" painters—first half of this century, particularly Felice Casorati and Giorgio De Chirico and Antonio Donghi. Second, the paintings of the Macchiaioli school—second half of the 19th century—the very best of these are Raffaello Sernesi's *Roofs in Sunlight* and Vincenzo Cabianca's *Peasant Woman at Montemurlo*, at least to my mind. Although these may not be the most important paintings in Rome, they are very good and because it's hard to see related work elsewhere, I really recommend a visit.
ANN HARTMAN
Artist

4.10 Villa Giulia / Museo Nazionale Etrusco
Villa designed by Vignola, et al., 1550–1555
Piazzale di Villa Giulia 9, ☎ 06 32 26 5 71

Stunning architecture housing an exceptional collection of Etruscan and ancient Greek art.
NANCY A. WINTER
Archaeologist

Built for Julius III (Giovanni del Monte) upon election in 1550, nominally under supervision of Michelangelo, the design owes much to Bramante and others, but in the sophisticated Mannerist taste of the 16th century. Reached by a wonderful walk through the Borghese Gardens, Villa Giulia now contains a great collection of Etruscan art. Like so much in Rome, it has layers of history and meaning.

Peter J. Holliday
Historian of classical art and archaeology, California State University–Long Beach

The villa house and garden are one—from the plan it is difficult to establish which is house and which is garden. The scale, the play of light and shadows, and the sheer simplicity make the Villa Giulia itself my favorite piece of art.

Peter G. Rolland
Landscape architect

A visit to the Museo Nazionale allows one to experience two distinctly different aspects of Rome at one time: the collection of funerary sculptural objects from the Etruscans, a proto-Roman civilization of 600 BC, set in Vignola's magnificent 16th-century villa built for Pope Julius III. While many of the Etruscan objects are reminiscent of Alberto Giacometti's 20th-century sculpture, the villa's garden is a Renaissance masterpiece of controlled vistas and pathways leading to a surprising spatial sequence involving nymphs and grottoes.

A similar experience would be to travel north of Rome to see the Etruscan tombs of Cerveteri and then Vignola's Villa Farnese in Caprarola.

Robert Evans
Architect

ALSO RECOMMENDED BY
Susan Kleinberg, Pamela Starr, John Kearney, Craig H. Walton

Sarcophagus of married couple
6th century BC

The Etruscan couple reclining on the couchlike cover of their sarcophagus are not a king and queen, but simply a

Obelisk stroll

It is worth surveying the imprint placed upon Rome at the end of the 16th century by Sixtus V, one of the greatest papal builders. It is no secret that Sixtus had a thing about obelisks (and straight streets that connect the principal papal basilicas). One of his first projects was to move the obelisk (brought to Rome from Alexandria in 37 AD) that stood beside St. Peter's to the piazza in front. In front of the loggia he had built at San Giovanni in Laterano, he placed an obelisk from the Circus Maximus. Looking out from the Lateran obelisk he built the very straight via Merulana that leads to Santa Maria Maggiore, where he was eventually buried. In front of Santa Maria Maggiore he erected another obelisk to mark the beginning of the street that runs to Trinità dei Monti, where there is yet another. Halfway along that street, another straight, and perpendicular, Sistine avenue leads southwest from the Porta Pia down to the Piazza del Quirinale, where there is another, by now inevitable, obelisk. From Trinità dei Monti you descend the Spanish Steps, and from the Piazza di Spagna look down the via del Babuino to the Piazza del Popolo, with its central obelisk. After a little detour to lunch at Otello off the via della Croce, you can walk down to the Popolo for coffee at Da Bolognese (Piazza del Popolo 1, at via di Ripetta, ☎ 06 36 123 76) and ponder how Sixtus sewed up the fabric of the city with his Egyptian needles.
VIRGINIA L. BUSH
Art historian

ITINERARY

- **a** St. Peter's Piazza San Pietro
- **b** San Giovanni in Laterano, Piazza San Giovanni in Laterano and via Merulana
- **c** Trinità dei Monti, at the top of the Spanish Steps
- **d** Piazza del Quirinale, via del Quirinale
- **e** Piazza del Popolo, via del Babuino and via del Corso

husband and wife, modest but proud. Their sarcophagus was found at Caere (Cerveteri), and the unknown sculptor or artisan was an Etruscan master able to execute in clay a complex piece that the modern potter would find extremely difficult to model and fire. There is not quite, but almost, a playful smile on their small pursed lips, as if they had some secret that only they can share.

NORMA GOLDMAN
Classicist, Wayne State University

ALSO RECOMMENDED BY
MARK ADAMS, ROBERT CAMPBELL, HELEN NAGY

RECOMMENDED READING 8

✗ Tavola Calda

Piazza Ungheria (not shown on map)

There's a good *tavola calda* on the Piazza Ungheria in the Parioli neighborhood—it doesn't even have a formal name. Inside is a cafeteria that serves some of the best food in Rome, especially the pasta at prices that will remind old hands of the days when Rome was a bargain. Your delicious meal can be eaten in the heated or air-conditioned interior depending on the season, or at outdoor tables under the plane trees in front of the establishment.

JOHN KENFIELD

PIAZZA DEL POPOLO AND VICINITY

4.11 Santa Maria del Popolo

Piazza del Popolo 12

Startling paintings, especially by Caravaggio, seen in a perfect setting. It is also nice to enter the church (and the piazza, actually) from such an interesting surrounding area. There is much else to see there as well, and a walk down the Corso to get there makes it even better.

LAWRENCE FANE
Sculptor

ALSO RECOMMENDED BY
THOMAS OBOE LEE, JON MICHAEL SCHWARTING

Crucifixion of Saint Peter and Conversion of Saint Paul
Caravaggio, 1600–1601

These are the most spectacular paintings that exist, I think, especially if one has any familiarity with the lives of Saints Peter and Paul. They are evocative, filled with violence and peace, acceptance and trust, consternation and fear. They're marvelous. Recently restored, they're also beautifully presented.

Christian Rome for two millennia has recognized Saints Peter and Paul as its "founders," its greatest saints. These paintings represent that, so if one were forced to choose one or two works that express a fundamentally Roman thing or characteristic, they could provide the example. Imagine them as companion pieces to the massive reliquaries holding the skulls of these saints in San Giovanni in Laterano, or the two spectacular basilicas on either side of the city, St. Peter's and San Paolo fuori le Mura.
KATHARINE BROPHY DUBOIS
Historian

Upon first seeing these two masterpieces side by side, you are surprised at the casual access you have to the actual paintings. They both emit a subtle warm light and their realism is startling. They were painted early in Caravaggio's career so their inner glow is strong and soothing. The foreshortening is amazing in *Conversion* and the dynamic composition of *Saint Peter* is very powerful.
FRANC PALAIA
Painter, photographer, muralist, curator

Astonishing depth created in a flat canvas; chiaroscuro at its best. The difficult viewing context heightens the delight of discovery and observation. An "essential" Roman experience involving smell (the musty air) and sight, and once again, just getting there engages the visitor with the rich context.
D. B. MIDDLETON
Architect

When you first enter Santa Maria del Popolo through scaffolding, sandbags, wires, and reconstruction machinery (it is alway *in restauro* whatever year you choose), you grope your way around in the dark for awhile vaguely depressed by the idea that here is another example of the Roman churches Eleanor Clark irreverently called "junk shops of idolatrous bric-a-brac." But if you find your way to the first chapel on the left of the choir and are fortunate enough to have a 500-lire coin, or even better, two or three, and locate the box into which to drop them—*ecco la luce!* At once the question arises: Where is the light coming from? In an annoying way you know it is from your 500-lire coin because a beam of it from up above is reflecting off the surface of the canvas making it almost impossible to see. But if you've taken an art history course and have been looking forward to seeing this painting ever since, you know there's another light, a transforming light coming from inside the work. Finally you see it under the horse where Paul is lying bathed in it with his arms open to it. This supernatural light is why you made the trip in the first place, and as an unlooked-for reward, you discover Caravaggio's *Crucifixion of Saint Peter* opposite. A miraculous light bathes Saint Peter as well, but despite (or maybe because of) the saint's being crucified upside down, the effect is not as persuasive as in the *Conversion of Saint Paul.*

JANET SULLIVAN
Writer, Rhode Island School of Design

ALSO RECOMMENDED BY
JOHN PECK, ROCÍO RODRÍGUEZ

RECOMMENDED READING 5, 17, 35, 42

4.12 **Vertecchi Stationery**

via della Croce 38 and across the street at via della Croce 70, ☎ 06 67 90 100, 06 67 83 110

This is a great school supply store—notebooks, pens, stationery, etc.

MARGARET BRUCIA

4.13   **Trattoria da Settimio all' Arancio**

via dell' Arancio 50. ☎ 06 68 76 119

RECOMMENDED BY
FRANCESCA SANTORO L'HOIR

4.14   **Augustan Monumental Complex**

Piazza Augusto Imperatore

Mausoleum
28 BC

Ara Pacis Augustae
13 BC

The sculpture of the Ara Pacis is to Rome what the Elgin
Marbles are to Athens. The relief sculptures of Aeneas, Tellus,
Augustus, the members of the Imperial family, and the
spectacular "inhabited" acanthus scroll are worth many visits
over a lifetime.
ROGER ULRICH
Classicist, Dartmouth College

Augustus' imprint on Rome was great—and much of it (and
his ideology) is reflected in this monument. The parallels
with Virgil's *Aeneid* are compelling and the connection with
Mussolini moves the antique world into the 20th century.
The continuity of the Ara Pacis fascinates me.
ANN THOMAS WILKINS
Classicist, Duquesne University

This may seem a strange recommendation, but the site effec-
tively highlights the crucial links between the "first" Roman
Empire, founded by Augustus, and the Fascist Empire
founded by Benito Mussolini, who so consciously and per-
sistently asserted the connection in support of his own
power.
  The piazza itself centers on the Mausoleum (28 BC), of
which only the base element, now well below street level,
still stands. Begun by Augustus as a funeral monument for
himself and his descendants, it did at one time hold the

remains not only of Augustus, but also of his family and some successors. The monument fell into ruin and was stripped of its ornament over the centuries and it was only fully excavated again in 1936–1938.

Mussolini's team also succeeded in disinterring and moving the Ara Pacis, which he chose to reconstruct at its present location, where its propaganda value was immense.

The altar proper is surrounded by a rectangular enclosure which forms part of what is called the Altar of Peace. The sculptural decoration is in bad condition, and scholars have argued about its meaning. Nonetheless, the depictions of religious ceremonies and, most especially, the participation of some noble Roman family (possibly Augustus' own) in those ceremonies, along with, perhaps, the old stories of Aeneas' sacrifice of the sow, and a depiction of Peace or Terra or the like in the form of an imposing female figure, clearly reflect the main lines of Augustus' religious and moral program.

The vast piazza was designed by Vittorio Ballio Morpurgo in 1937–1940 specifically for purposes of housing the ancient monumental complex. Its surrounding architecture is typically Fascist in style, revising the models from classical antiquity for its own intimidating purposes. (The original Roman restaurant Alfredo's is located in one of the huge, cold arcades which front the piazza.)

To visit the Piazza Augusto Imperatore is to peer into architectural propaganda at its most powerful. Both Augustus and Mussolini were masters of propaganda in all of its forms, and here the masters meet to compare notes—and facts.
LINDA W. RUTLAND GILLISON
Classicist, University of Montana

A very refined distillation of the spirit and history of Classical Rome.
CATHERINE SPOTSWOOD GIBBES
Classical scholar, linguist, researcher, Hebrew College

ALSO RECOMMENDED BY
URSULA HEIBGES

RECOMMENDED READING 14, 16, 64, 83

4.15 Outdoor Print Market

Largo Fontanella Borghese
closed Monday

The open-air print market is near via dell'Arancio. Old printed views of Rome, vintage postcards, 1930s black and white photographs, botanical prints, hand-colored maps with marvelously detailed borders, and assorted ephemera can be found at the stalls. Piranesi prints galore—no first editions, but some fairly good-quality prints created from his 1,000 engravings of the *Vedute di Roma*.
JOHN JAY STONEHILL AND JUDITH STONEHILL

4.16 Buca di Ripetta

via di Ripetta 36, ☎ 06 32 29 391

No explanation needed, for those who go. Roman food in a Roman setting.
ROBERT MCCARTER

THE VATICAN

AND

CASTEL SANT'ANGELO

5

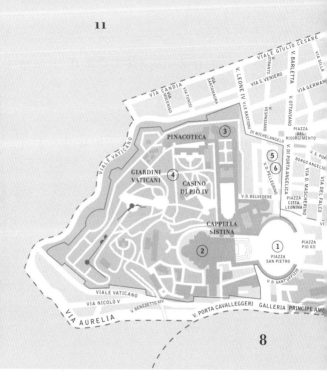

8

ST. PETER'S BASILICA AND PIAZZA

1. Piazza and Colonnade
2. St. Peter's Basilica

VATICAN MUSEUMS AND GARDENS

Access to all the Vatican Museums, including the Sistine Chapel and the Raphael Rooms, is through one entrance on viale Vaticano, shown on map 5 as ③.

3. Sistine Chapel
   Scala Regia

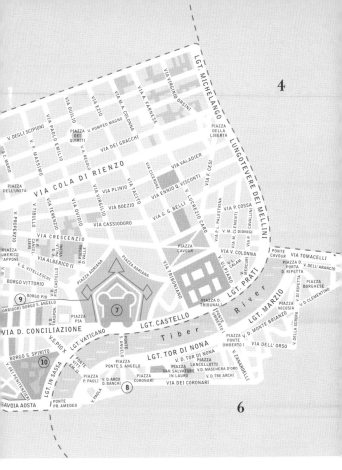

N

ST. PETER'S BASILICA AND PIAZZA

The greatest architects and the most gifted artists of the
Counter-Reformation and the Baroque came to make an
unprecedented masterpiece of theater, art, and architecture.
RICHARD MEIER
Architect

In Rome, it's important to see things "right" the first time:
a first-time visitor should under no circumstances approach
St. Peter's Basilica along Mussolini's hideous via della
Conciliazione, but should enter Piazza San Pietro through
the side colonnades, and be properly surprised by the huge
space and spectacular façade.
SUSAN WOOD
Art historian, Oakland University

5.1 ## Piazza and Colonnade

Bernini, 1656–1667

The Piazza San Pietro engages the informed viewer in a fascinating visual dialogue about space and how perspective
manipulations can influence spatial experience. The piazza,
which is partly enclosed by two semicircular colonnades,
has the form of an ellipse. From either of the foci of the
elliptical piazza, the nearest four-row colonnade appears
only one column deep. From any other vantage point, this
visibility beyond the colonnade gives way to a virtual forest
of columns. The contrast is dramatic. The other perspective
manipulation in the piazza corrects what was thought to be
a disproportionally elongated church façade. A long ramp,
inserted in the middle of the great staircase which leads up
to the portico of the basilica, extends almost directly to the
front stairs of the church. Because the viewer on the piazza
floor cannot see the ramp and the actual space covered by it,
the stairs visually flatten and appear to widen the plane of
the church façade. In both of these examples, Bernini
challenges his audience to elevate their consciousness by
reflecting on the process of spatial perception.
DAVID LAPALOMBARA
Artist, Antioch College

Watch out for the pigeons! The scale of this work is absolutely surprising—an interesting and ingenious solution of visual lead-in to St. Peter's.

Gianne Harper
Artist and painter

The scale, the light, and shadow play are magnificent, to say nothing of the details. The curved ramp steps at the entry are one detail not to be missed. Check out how the whole piazza drains: all the rainwater flows to the base of the four light standards surrounding the Egyptian obelisk. If one stands at a certain point marked on the pavement near the obelisk the colonnade seems to have only one row of columns.

Peter G. Rolland
Landscape architect

5.2 St. Peter's Basilica

Bramante, Raphael, Giuliano da Sangallo, Baldassare Peruzzi, Antonio da Sangallo, Michelangelo, Carlo da Maderno, Bernini, Giacomo da Pietrosanta, Pirro Ligorio, Domenico Fontana, Giuseppe Momo, Luca Beltrami, etc.

St. Peter's is a résumé of so much that is Roman, from Michelangelo's *Pietà* to Bernini's Baldacchino and Cathedra Petri and Giotto's mosaic of the Navicella. Its outsized dimensions and grandiose decoration are overwhelming, making the experience of walking through the building a dynamic one. The tombs of the popes provide a visual history of art and of the papacy.

Bruce Boucher
Art historian, University College, London

St. Peter's Basilica is the reason why Rome is still the center of the civilized world. For religious, historical, and architectural reasons it by itself justifies a journey to Rome, and its interior offers a palimpsest of artistic styles at their best—e.g., Bernini's great tomb for Pope Alexander VII, Michelangelo's *Pietà*, the Baldacchino, and the dome. Down below, the pagan necropolis in the *scavi* and the tomb of

Saint Peter should not be missed.
HELEN F. NORTH
Classicist, Swarthmore College

I find the interior of St. Peter's and the Vatican Museum overbearing and a bit creepy but it certainly tells the story of power. And difficult as it is to make your way to the Sistine Chapel, it is one of the miracles.
LAWRENCE FANE
Sculptor

The full strength of the Church is most palpable in this one building, even though others, such as Santa Costanza, are more gentle on the spirit. Be there when it opens. The crowds build quickly. The view from the roof and the dome above is breathtaking.
STEVEN BROOKE
Architectural photographer and writer

Visitors should take time to comprehend the enormous vault of the building and compare it to such ruined basilicas as that of Constantine in the Forum.
JAMES M. LATTIS
Historian of Astronomy, University of Wisconsin–Madison

ALSO RECOMMENDED BY
JANIS BELL, ALDO CASANOVA, PAUL CLOGAN, MICHAEL CONFORTI, CORNELIA AND LUKAS FOSS, JOHN KEARNEY, STUART M. MERTZ, THEODORE K. RABB, THOMAS H. WATKINS, CHARLES K. WILLIAMS II, JOHN L. WONG

Pietà
Michelangelo, 1499

Incontournable, a true *chef d'oeuvre* with such tenderness and empathy—a miracle that these ephemeral states be so perfectly communicated in the hardness of stone. Go early or just before closing to be alone with this work.
GIANNE HARPER
Artist and painter

There are works of art—Leonardo da Vinci's *Mona Lisa* and Rembrandt's *Christ at Emmaus* in the Louvre among

NAMES OF ROME

The area north of Trastevere has been called the Vatican from the earliest days. The word is of unknown significance, probably a Romanized version of the name of an Etruscan settlement that has left no other trace. The etymology of the name was already a matter of concern among ancient scholars. One of them connects it with the name of a deity who presided over the first sound made by infants (va in Latin was pronounced "wa"). To the ancient Romans, the ager Vaticanus, "Vatican field" was notorious as the source of a much-maligned cheap wine.

PAUL PASCAL
Classicist, University of Washington

them—which set the standard for all other works of art. Michelangelo's *Pietà* in St. Peter's is undoubtedly one of these incomparable creations. The statue is of extraordinary importance in the career of the artist. Before this Pietà Michelangelo's output in Florence and Bologna had been of but minor significance. He had been in Rome three years when, in 1499, the French Cardinal Jean de Bilhères de Langraulas commissioned the *Pietà*. It was with this statue that the artist's genius became manifest. Of flawless white Carrara marble, the composition shows the dead Christ lying across his mother's lap. His hand, pierced by a nail, at once an emblem of suffering and salvation, is the part of his body nearest the viewer. The Virgin, whose flowing robes are both comforter and shroud, stretches out her left hand in an eloquent gesture which cries out to the whole world: "Look what you have done!" Surprisingly, her face is not that of a woman well past middle age, as would befit a mother with a son in his thirties. Instead, with his overwhelming love of beauty, the artist has chosen to portray Mary as a young and lovely woman whose physical beauty reflects the beauty of her soul. Upon the ribbon which stretches across the Madonna's breast, the twenty-five-year-old artist boldly inscribed his name for all to see: *Michaelangelus Bonarotus*

Florent. Faciebat. He was proud of this work. Here, in
mourning and beauty, his great career begins.
DAVID GARRARD LOWE
Art historian, author

Terribly moving, emotional. Viewers, including myself,
simply stood in silence for a very long time, absorbing the
deep sadness of the sculpture and appreciating the weight
and grace of the material that makes the figures.
SUSAN MOLESKY
Architectural designer

It's perfect, yet so fragile. So accessible, yet screened by a
glass because of a madman. A symbol of the human potential, yet it displays our capacity to inflict misery. The *Pietà* is
smaller than I imagined, but has lingered longer in my mind
than I expected.
FREDERICK STEINER
*Professor of planning and landscape architecture, Arizona
State University*

ALSO RECOMMENDED BY:
FRANCES BLANK, ALDO CASANOVA, CORNELIA AND LUKAS
FOSS, BARBARA GOLDSMITH, MILLER HORNS, HELEN
NORTH, REBECCA WEST, JOHN L. WONG

Baldacchino
Bernini, 1633

There are so many Romes in Rome that exist side by side or
on top of each other in layers, that the problem is always one
of focus.

One of my favorites is the frieze around Bernini's altar
in St. Peter's. With your back to the main entrance, stand at
the left column. Look at the base just below eye level and
find the face of a woman in pain. Track her progress around
the base, watching the agony grow at each tablet; you are
seeing a woman in childbirth. At the base of the last pillar,
an infant's beatifically smiling face emerges out of the stone.
Why is it there? I don't know.
JOHN GUARE
Playwright

A visit to St. Peter's in the later afternoon provides instant access to the scenographic values of Baroque art. Light combines with gilded bronze to ennoble the sculptural program of the immense reliquary, conferring a solidity of faith to match the immense setting of the basilica. On making one's way to Bernini's Altar of the Chair deep in the apse one is also encouraged to visit Michelangelo's *Pietà* in the right aisle, as well as other notable artworks and architecture.

CHARLES WITKE
Classicist, University of Michigan

Unequaled scale of an altar situation. The Pope's locus, during services.

GARY R. HILDERBRAND
Landscape architect

ALSO RECOMMENDED BY
ALDO CASANOVA, MARTIE HOLMER, HENRY MIRICK,
HELEN NORTH

Statue of Saint Peter
Arnolfo di Cambio, c. 1296

Originally housed in Constantine's basilica at San Giovanni in Laterano and moved to the present church, this late Gothic image of the apostle and first pope is not so remarkable as a work of art as it is as an object of veneration. The extended right foot of the bronze figure has been worn smooth by centuries of devotions by the faithful, and on great feasts it is dressed in sumptuous robes and a papal mitre. It is an eloquent reminder of Rome as first and foremost a place of pilgrimage.

MARTIN FILLER
Architecture critic and curator

ALSO RECOMMENDED BY
ANDREA CALLARD, GERDA S. PANOFSKY, PIKE POWERS,
CHARLES WUORINEN

RECOMMENDED READING 54

Tomb of Alexander VII
Bernini, 1678

To my mind, this is one of the most moving pieces in the entire Vatican. The powerful juxtaposition between the pale, cool pontiff (with his accompanying virtues: Justice, Prudence, Charity, and Truth) and the fiercely Baroque Death (a gilt skeleton rearing up from under a richly colored marble shroud) offers both a reminder of man's mortality and the promise of ultimate transcendence. The execution itself, especially the enshrouded Death, is absolutely stunning.
R.J.W. CRO
Art historian and archaeologist, Princeton University

ALSO RECOMMENDED BY
HELEN NORTH

Stoup for Holy Water, with putti
Bernini

This is on the first pier on the right, as you enter the nave. Voluptuous use of marble.
ROBERT LIVESEY
Architect, Director of Knowlton School of Architecture, Ohio State University

The Scavi: Necropolis and Saint Peter's Tomb
1st to 3rd century AD
Permission may be obtained by applying in writing or in person to the Ufficio Scavi (beneath the Arco della Campana to the left of St. Peter's), open 9–7. ☎ *06 69 88 53 18*

You'll be assigned to a group of fifteen and a tour guide (specify language), who details the incredible history of the space, including an explanation of why, in engineering terms, the basilica was built in the wrong place. Don't forget, when you reach Saint Peter's tomb, to ask the tour guide if Peter really is buried there. The answer might surprise you.
MATTHEW GELLER
Artist

There is no better or more literal way to experience the
sense of Rome as a multilayered accretion of history than to
visit the archaeological excavations beneath the Basilica of
St. Peter. As one moves successively downward from the
Baroque church to the Romanesque sanctuary and finally to
the Roman cemetery and the tomb of the apostle, one is
filled with an overwhelming realization of the weight of the
past and the inescapable fact that one's own epoch will
become simply another stratum in the great pile-up of time.

MARTIN FILLER
Architecture critic and curator

ALSO RECOMMENDED BY
ANDREA CALLARD, KENNETH D. S. LAPATIN, HELEN NORTH,
GERDA S. PANOFSKY, PIKE POWERS, CHARLES WUORINEN

VATICAN MUSEUMS AND GARDENS

*Access to all the Vatican Museums, including the Sistine
Chapel and the Raphael Rooms, is through one entrance
on viale Vaticano, shown on map 5 as ③.*

5.3   ## Sistine Chapel

Michelangelo, 1508-1512

Go one hour before the Vatican opens to be one of the first
in line. Buy a ticket, pass everything by, continue through
the Gallery of Maps, skipping the Raphael Stanze. Head
directly down the steep stairs to the chapel. You will be there
twenty to thirty minutes ahead of the crowd. Then, enjoy the
privacy of one of the sublime expressions of human longing
for comprehension of the cosmos.

WILLIAM WYER
Rare book seller

I had the rare opportunity of being alone (well, almost
alone—three or four others were also in the chapel) when
Bach was being played. It was not religiously impressive or
affecting, but inspirational; its sheer dimensions and the
quality of the experience were fantastic. As Vasari said, "He

brought the blessing of light to the painting, which sufficed
to illuminate a world plunged in darkness for centuries."
RICHARD MEIER
Architect

If you can be there when it's not crowded, try to get away
with lying down on the floor to look up at it.
JON MICHAEL SCHWARTING
Architect, New York Institute of Technology

Be first in line, go (sprint) to the chapel directly, bring
binoculars. It will be quiet and relatively uncrowded for at
least thirty minutes. The magnitude of this accomplishment—and the sheer force of both artistic and papal
power—is simply unequaled. When finished, work your way
back past Raphael's *School of Athens*.
STEVEN BROOKE
Architectural photographer and writer

Amazing use of color to show form to be viewed at sixty-foot
heights. The most saturated hues are used as receding forms
and the advancing forms are the lightest in value. Raphael
did not use color as a structural tool. Michelangelo is unique.
MARJORIE KREILICK
Artist, University of Wisconsin

Wall frescoes by Botticelli, Perugino, Domenico, Ghirlandaio,
Cosimo Rosselli, Pinturicchio, and others.
JOHN LENAGHAN
Historian, Rutgers University

Visiting the Sistine Chapel requires one to walk through the
entire length of the Vatican Museums, and along the way,
see a lot of other great works, including some that directly
influenced Michelangelo, like the *Laocoön* group and the
Belvedere Torso. Do not miss the lovely little chapel by Fra
Angelico, which many visitors pass en route to the Raphael
Stanze without even knowing it's there; catch the Odyssey
Landscape frescoes in the Vatican Library on the way out.
SUSAN WOOD
Art historian, Oakland University

ALSO RECOMMENDED BY

KIMBERLY ACKERT, LIDIA MATTICCHIO BASTIANICH,
AL BLAUSTEIN, THOMAS L. BOSWORTH, ROBERT CAMPBELL,
CAREN CANIER, JENNY STRAUSS CLAY, MICHAEL CONFORTI,
RICHARD FRANK, KATHERINE GEFFCKEN, URSULA HEIBGES,
MILLER HORNS, J. RICHARD JUDSON, LYNN KEARNEY,
HARDU KECK, BENJAMIN KOHL, DAVID LAPALOMBARA,
JOHN C. LEAVEY, EUGENE (GENE) E. MATTHEWS, ROBERT
MCCARTER, JAMES H. S. MCGREGOR, SUSAN MOLESKY,
GERDA S. PANOFSKY, ERNST PULGRAM, LESLIE RAINER,
ANTON RAJER, ROCÍO RODRÍGUEZ, PETER G. ROLLAND,
MICHELE RENEE SALZMAN, SUSAN SILBERBERG-PEIRCE,
PAMELA STARR, JUNE N. STUBBS AND JOHN C. STUBBS,
JANET SULLIVAN, JOHN H. THOW, JOHN VARRIANO,
EMILY M. WHITESIDE, CHARLES K. WILLIAMS II,
NANCY A. WINTER

RECOMMENDED READING 11, 23, 26, 27, 33, 48, 60, 78, 81

5.3 Scala Regia

Bernini, 1663-1666

A must-see. Another powerful architectural space; triple
perspectives; a walk up the stair is like walking to heaven to
meet the gods.
JOHN L. WONG
Landscape architect

🛢 LOLLI-POPES

It may sound kinky to offer a friend the chance to lick
the Pope into oblivion, but the tasteful six-inch lollipops
with the Pope's face emblazoned on them that are for
sale in the Vatican stores are His Holiness-approved.
For the innocents, there are T-shirts.
JAYNE MERKEL

5.3 Stanza della Segnatura

in the Raphael Rooms

Despite the crowds and convoluted access route, once you arrive, you'll feel transported to a strange, ideal, High Renaissance world. This complete sequence of classically ordered, consummately crafted, rigorously representational frescoes covers all four walls of the first room Raphael decorated for Pope Julius II. Using the vanishing point perspective, sculpturesque modeling, and other new illusionistic techniques, the artist created figures, sculpture, and architecture in paint, not purely for decorative purposes but to depict the Neoplatonic view of the achievements of the human spirit. The four frescoes represent the School of Athens (philosophy), Disputation over the Sacrament, the Cardinal and Theological Virtues, and Parnassus. The idea of summing up all knowledge and belief may seem simplistic to the contemporary mind, but there is nothing simple about the way it was done here. Form and content have rarely found a better fit or been achieved on a higher level. But confidence in man's ability to know all didn't last long, as a visit to the adjoining rooms—also well worth the journey—shows.

JAYNE MERKEL
Art historian and critic

Wandering the endless color-coded visitor paths of the Vatican Museums is both trying and disorienting. The best of art and architecture is blurred by the crowds and the sheer vastness of the collection. Take a detour from the rather short "Brown" tour to see this incredible group of paintings and frescoes. The power of the images is in their varied emotional and intellectual content and in the intimacy of the room's scale. The delicacy of the coloring is superb. Think about these rooms being completed at the same time as Michelangelo's work on the Sistine Chapel.

WENDY EVANS JOSEPH
Architect

Fresco of the School of Athens
Raphael, 1508–1511

If one image could explain Renaissance Rome, this is it, still more than the Sistine Chapel ceiling; for here the wisdom of ancient philosophers is incorporated into a vision of God's plan for the cosmos in such a way as to embrace every time and every creed. The people in Raphael's fresco, moreover, represent living books—this room was the private library of Pope Julius II, and we can presume that cupboards with philosophical books were arranged along the lower wall beneath Raphael's fresco. Raphael is probably the most technically brilliant fresco painter who ever lived.

INGRID D. ROWLAND
Historian, University of Chicago

A Renaissance painter depicts a Roman setting for a Greek subject. The painting demonstrates the incredible compression which has occurred in Mediterranean culture throughout history. Rather than viewing this culture as discrete elements over time, we see it as a single continuum.

WALTER CHATHAM
Architect

RECOMMENDED READING 36, 85

ALSO RECOMMENDED BY
JAMES H. S. McGREGOR, DAVID ST. JOHN, A. RICHARD
WILLIAMS

Fresco of Parnassus
Raphael, 1508–1511

Its extraordinary yet friendly gallery/catalog of visionaries and poets helps to locate me as to my own tiny talent.

DAVID ST. JOHN
Poet, University of Southern California

5.3 ## Stanza d'Eliodoro

in the Raphael Rooms

Fresco of the Mass of Bolsena
Raphael, 1512–1514

This beautiful fresco can be viewed as: a pious scene of

devout worship; or an elaborately staged spectacle with participants who are shrewd men of the world. Note the tension between the face of Pope Julius II, who appears transcendent, and the rings on his praying fingers—the dilemma of Rome at a glance!

Walter Chatham
Architect

RECOMMENDED READING 44

5.3 Chapel of Nicholas V

Frescoes by Fra Angelico, 1447–1451

Tiny jewel-like scenes from the lives of Saint Stephen and Saint Lawrence.

Lynn Kearney
Artist, curator

5.3 Pinacoteca / Vatican Picture Galleries

Stefaneschi Altarpiece
Giotto and assistants, c. 1315
in Room II

Three panels originally on the high altar of St. Peter's.

Lynn Kearney

Sixtus IV Receiving Platina
Melozzo da Forli, 1477
in Room IV

RECOMMENDED BY
Lynn Kearney

Madonna of Foligno
Raphael, 1512
in Room VII

RECOMMENDED BY
Henry D. Mirick
Architect

Last Communion of Saint Jerome
Domenichino, 1615
in Room XII

…for its subtle lighting, exquisite coloring, moving rendition of the last breath of the aged hermit Saint Jerome, and beautiful visage of a young acolyte. Compare it with Raphael's *Transfiguration* in a nearby room. Poussin thought these were the greatest paintings ever painted.
Janis Bell
Holistic educator and spiritual healer, art historian

RECOMMENDED READING 89

Deposition
Caravaggio, 1604
in Room XII

RECOMMENDED BY
John L. Wong
Landscape architect

Transfiguration of Christ
Raphael, 1520

RECOMMENDED BY
Thomas Gordon Smith

5.3 Museums of Antiquities

The first-time visitor should linger in the vast galleries of the Vatican Museums. There will be little competition for space in front of masterpieces like the Augustus of Prima Porta or the Odyssey Landscapes.
Roger Ulrich
Classicist, Dartmouth College

Laocoön
c. 150 BC
in the Octagonal Courtyard

Great Hellenistic statue influential on Michelangelo, et al.
H. ALAN SHAPIRO
Classicist, Johns Hopkins University

The *Laocoön* is one of the most dramatic and beautifully crafted marble sculptures from Greco-Roman antiquity. The emotion, refinement of carving, and excitement of the piece are truly remarkable and memorable. It was probably the work of three sculptors from the school of Rhodes and was undoubtedly seen by Michelangelo during the Renaissance.
SUSAN SILBERBERG-PEIRCE
Art historian, Colorado State University

ALSO RECOMMENDED BY
IAIN LOW

RECOMMENDED READING 79

Prima Porta Augustus
in the Braccio Nuovo

RECOMMENDED BY
JOHN LENAGHAN
Historian, Rutgers University

Try to wend your way through the Vatican hierarchy and get those difficult-to-secure permissions, for St. Peter's, and its environment, is filled with the most unexpected things. For example, the Church went on a "defacement" campaign of all the ancient male nude statues they came across. But, tyranny being in the details, all the details have been saved, stored in the Vatican, trophies from the Christian victory over the pagans. A German art historian has been studying them for years in order to establish provenance.
PIER CONSAGRA
Artist

5.3 ## Other Galleries

Skip the modern religious art—the quantity-to-quality ratio
is like no other museum in the world. The Gallery of Maps
is altogether another, happier, story.
MATTHEW GELLER
Artist

The Kiss of Judas
Karl Schmidt-Rottluff, 1918
in the Gallery of Modern Religious Art

The visitor cannot go too early nor stay too late among these
powerful works of Christendom. For me *The Kiss of Judas* is
as moving as any. Though modest in size (15" x 19") and
showing only the heads of the two protagonists, we are left
with Judas to share in the traitor's guilt as Jesus stares in
sorrow. The collection as a whole nearly overwhelms.
JAMES R. TURNER
Landscape architect

Sancta Sanctorum Treasure
in the Chapel of Pius V

This is the treasure deposited in the altar of the Sancta
Sanctorum in the Lateran Palace by Pope Leo III at the beginning of the 9th century and added to by later medieval popes.
Sealed until 1903, when it was opened by Leo XIII, the chest
of treasure yielded a remarkable group of early Christian
Byzantine and medieval relics and reliquaries, many of them
unique. The two dozen objects are the Vatican's greatest
medieval holdings. Often unnoticed because of the installation and poor lighting.
ROBERT P. BERGMAN (1945–1999)
Director, Cleveland Museum of Art (1993–1999)

Black figure amphora
Exekias, c. 540 BC
in the Etruscan Museum

One of the three or four finest Greek vases in existence.
H. ALAN SHAPIRO
Classicist, Johns Hopkins University

5.4 Vatican Gardens

Call several days in advance, ☎ 06 69 88 44 66

The Vatican Gardens behind St. Peter's are full of fantastic views and fountains, a treasure to walk through. The view of St. Peter's from the back—especially the dome—is thrilling. The Casina, or summer house, of Pius IV is amazing.
JOHN KEARNEY
Sculptor

RECOMMENDED READING 1

Casina of Pius IV
Pirro Ligorio, 1558-1562

A world within a world, the perfect harmony of the oval court with its four templelike gates defines a place of meditation and peace. Surrounded by tall pines and greenery, with the dome of St. Peter's looming beyond, floating dreamlike above the horizon, it's a microcosm of the city with its piazzas and domed churches.
ALEXANDER GORLIN
Architect

This charming pair of buildings was built for the Pope to cavort in. They are so very different in tone and feeling from the rest of the Vatican, and are fine expressions of the architecture of pleasure in a city famous for showing a pious face while hiding the sensual behind walls—"private" Rome at its most accessible.
WALTER CHATHAM
Architect

5.5 Bar Santa Anna

✕ via Santa Anna, across the street from the Vatican and St. Peter's, just before the viale della Porta Angelica (one block north of St. Peter's)

For lunch, really first-rate sandwiches are served here, and you can sit down and eat at a table for not much more than bar prices.
PAMELA STARR

5.6 Pizzeria il Migliore

X via Santa Anna, about 3½ blocks down from the bar of the same name

This pizza stand offers an incredible variety of pizza slices sold by the *etto* (100 grams). Take your pizza to the nearby park surrounding the Castel Sant'Angelo (where Tosca jumped off).

Pamela Starr

CASTEL SANT'ANGELO AND THE BORGO

5.7 Castel Sant'Angelo

Hadrian, 128 AD, with medieval and Renaissance additions

☎ 06 68 75 036

The complex variety of historic settings—prison, tomb, apartments, fortress—makes this a "something for everyone" pilgrimage. Adults, scholars, and children respond to its mystique: Beatrice Cenci, who, with her mother and brother, was beheaded on the Ponte; popes alerted and escaping here from the Vatican; and Cellini dueling on the open walk. Inside, the splendid paintings of the rooms and their adornments contrast with the dank dungeons.

Robert G. Hamilton
Painter

...full of history and intrigue. There are instruments of torture, and interesting quarters for the popes, with revealing
X frescoes. Have lunch up on top for a spectacular view.

John Kearney
Sculptor

...for the opera lover.

Frances Blank
Fellow of the American Academy in Rome, 1940, Classics and Archaeology

To St. Peter's with Bernini

The first-time visitor to Rome should go
to St. Peter's, but not the way most people
do, which is up the anachronistic Corso
Vittorio Emanuele and then up Mussolini's
via della Conciliazione. Rather, go the way
Bernini might have gone to work there.
Starting perhaps with Mass at San Giovanni
dei Fiorentini, cross the piazza and wind
through the tiny via Paola to the Ponte
Sant'Angelo, the only ancient crossing over
the Tiber in this part of the city. Passing
between the 16th-century guardian figures
of Peter and Paul and admiring the Bernini-
designed angels on either side, one can look
up to the top of the Castello and give thanks
to the image of Saint Michael, protector of
the city. Pass around to the left and follow
the elevated corridor that connects the
fortress with the Vatican Palace, enabling
popes to take refuge in the Castello in
times of siege. Then, and only then, plunge
through Bernini's Colonnade, so that the
expanse of the piazza and the splendor of
the façade and Michelangelo's dome come
as the stunning, theatrical surprise that
Bernini intended.

VIRGINIA L. BUSH
Art historian

ITINERARY

a San Giovanni dei
Fiorentini, at via
Giulia and Piazza
d'Oro

b Ponte Sant'Angelo

c Vatican Corridor,
Borgo Sant'Angelo
to via dei Corridori

d Bernini's Colonnade,
Piazza San Pietro

The procession up the dark, forboding ramp, followed by the explosion of light and views at the top, is breathtaking. The rooms decorated by Giulio Romano are as cheerful as anything in Rome—ironic, since they were to house the Pope in time of siege. The views across Rome are superb and there is a small café adjacent in a courtyard on the roof.

WALTER CHATHAM
Architect

ALSO RECOMMENDED BY
ANDREA CALLARD, GIANNE HARPER, JOHN VARRIANO

RECOMMENDED READING 15, 38, 55, 88, 115

5.8 La Taverna da Giovanni

via Banco di Santo Spirito 58, directly across the bridge from Castel Sant'Angelo, ☎ 06 68 61 512

Here is the family-run trattoria where I learned about the simple wonders of the Italian table. Giovanni has sadly passed away, but his son Mimmo proudly holds court. La Taverna's clientele is a cross section of loyal locals and an occasional tourbus-load of Germans. But the honest kitchen run by Claudio is the reason to dine here. Just ask Mimmo to take care of you. Savor Roman antipasti, pasta (ask for *bombolotti "al modo mio"*), and the best roast lamb and pork (*maialino*). Finish with a swig of potent *centerbe*—the house *digestivo* infused with "a hundred herbs."

DANNY MEYER

5.9 The Borgo

The Borgo district near St. Peter's was the old papal citadel and was populated by the first pilgrims to visit the site of Peter's martyrdom at Nero's Circus. In 850 AD, Pope Leo VII built the forty-foot walls that still surround the neighborhood. Today, the neighborhood thrives, serving the needs of the pilgrims and tourists who come to St. Peter's and move to the rhythm of its bells. They spill over into the Borgo's restaurants, cafés, and religious vestment shops.

No foreign invader wreaked as much havoc on the Borgo as Mussolini's urban designers, whose construction of the triumphal via della Conciliazione cut through the heart of the medieval neighborhood. Today's visitor to Castel Sant'Angelo and St. Peter's can easily overlook the district when approaching via the parade route. Slip inside the wall behind the Renaissance Palazzo Torlonia and have coffee at the marble bar at Sclianga to watch the Borgo Pio street life. Walk along Borgo Pio and sample three of Rome's acquas at fountains along the street and the local piazza. Borgo Pio leads to via Porta Angelica which runs along the Vatican walls from St. Peter's to the treasure houses of the Vatican Museums.

TODD STONE
Artist

5.10 **Museo Storico Nazionale dell'Arte Sanitaria**

Santo Spirito Hospital
Lungotevere in Sassia 3, ☎ 06 68 35 2353

Full of medieval medical equipment, memento mori, and then one whole section of all sorts of birth anomalies. If the Cappuccini mummies at Santa Maria della Concezione get boring, try this one! Open to the public but only by appointment.

MARY ANN MELCHERT
American Academy in Rome, 1984–1988

ALSO RECOMMENDED BY
GERALDINE ERMAN

THE PANTHEON,

CAMPO MARZIO

AND

PIAZZA NAVONA

6

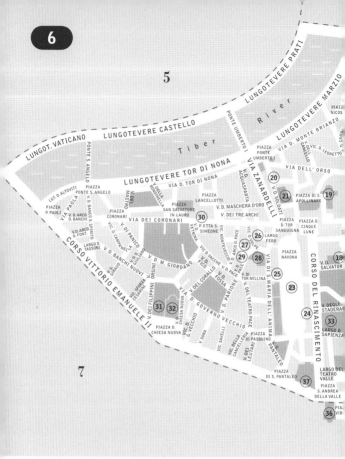

N

THE PANTHEON AND VICINITY

6.1   ## Palazzo Doria Pamphili

Piazza del Collegio Romano 1a,   ☎ 06 67 97 323

For a very simple, yet utterly breathtaking effect, visit in winter, at dusk, and contrive to be in the galleries when they turn the lights on. We entered the galleries in the middle of a February afternoon, wandering and marveling at the sumptuous rooms and corridors. As we turned to retrace our steps to the exit we found that the darkening galleries had been lit with endless crystal chandeliers and sparkling wall sconces. (About light in Rome, Augustus Hare in *Walks in Rome* gives a list of the best places for morning and afternoon light.)
PAMELA KEECH
Sculptor, installation artist, historian

Perfect early Roman private collection and one of the few remaining intact anywhere.
MICHAEL CONFORTI
Director, Clark Art Institute, Williamstown MA

Portrait of Pope Innocent X
Velázquez, 1650

My favorite painting / sculpture in Rome.
ROBERT CAMPBELL
Architect, writer, Pulitzer Prize for criticism (1996)

The greatest single painting in Rome.
JOHN C. LEAVEY
Painter

It is a stunning experience to come so close to this masterpiece in this surrounding. An elegant setting with three Caravaggios on one wall as well.
ROBERT G. HAMILTON
Painter

I can't be in Rome without going to see this portrait. The approach is dramatic: one first sees the reflection of the portrait in the mirrored doorway of the room it shares with

Bernini's bust of Innocent X. Entering the room one sees
only Bernini's very noble idealized portrait before turning
and facing the Velázquez. The painting combines penetrating,
unidealized portraiture and dazzling painterly virtuosity—
and brilliant, shining crimson satin with frothy whites—in
the traditional enobling format (since Raphael) for papal
portraiture.
JEAN WEISZ
Art historian, University of California–Los Angeles

Rest on the Flight into Egypt
Caravaggio, c. 1595

RECOMMENDED BY
JENNY STRAUSS CLAY
Classicist, University of Virginia

6.2 Sant'Ignazio

Orazio Grassi, Alessandro Algardi, 1626–1650
Piazza di Sant'Ignazio

Wonderful *trompe l'oeil* ceiling frescoes, vertiginous
perspectives; bring change for the coin-operated ceiling
illumination.
HARVEY SOLLBERGER
*Composer, conductor, Music Director of the La Jolla
Symphony Orchestra*

Stand on the strategically placed stars in the pavement of
the nave. On the first star, look at the vaulted ceiling, and
then at the "cupola" with the beam of light sifting through
one window. Then look at the floor while you walk to the
star under the cupola. Now look up: the cupola has collapsed.
It's only paint applied to the ceiling—*trompe l'oeil*. You can
do the same thing under the central fresco. If you walk to a
corner the entire ceiling tilts. Then go outside to the piazza
with its "scenery," "entrances," and "exits"—it's a stage setting, and the people in the piazza are the actors.
FRANCESCA SANTORO L'HOIR
Classicist

Two spectacular ceiling paintings just a couple of blocks away from each other are good for a comparative look. The first is Andrea Pozzo's extraordinary fresco in the church of Sant'Ignazio. It's particularly interesting for Americans to see his Indian in full headdress which was as exotic to the late 17th-century viewer as a landscape from Mars would be today.

The same church also contains Pozzo's *trompe l'oeil* cupola, painted in the 1680s. Its illusion is most perfectly seen from a marked stone on the floor. Pozzo's treatise on perspective raced through Europe in successive editions through the next half-century and influenced architects and painters everywhere.

Two blocks away, in the Gesù church, is another great ceiling painting by G. B. Gaulli (also called Baciccia). This and the earlier ceiling should give anyone an understanding of Baroque Rome. There is another smaller-scale *trompe l'oeil* by Pozzo in the rooms of St. Ignatius (see below).

VINCENT BUONANNO
Book collector

ALSO RECOMMENDED BY
JANIS BELL, PAMELA STARR, A. RICHARD WILLIAMS

6.3   Rooms of St. Ignatius
Piazza del Gesù 45

The Pozzo Corridor
Andrea Pozzo, 1680s

A wonderful example of perspective painting on a small and accessible scale. Only by walking down the corridor does one realize the extent of the distortion necessary to create proper perspective. My children (who were seven and eleven years old) called it "The Holy Fun House."

MARGARET BRUCIA
Classicist

6.4   Piazza di Sant'Ignazio
Filippo Raguzzini, 1728

Filippo Raguzzini built the three shallow buildings separated

by the wings of narrow streets as a Rococo theater set where
various people participate as "actors" and/or "spectators"
involved in their daily routines, creating urban operas free
of charge.

Emily M. Whiteside
Consultant on the arts, preservation, and design

6.5 Due Colonne Ristorante

✗ via del Seminario 122, just off Piazza di
Sant'Ignazio

A great restaurant, moderately priced, on the street that
connects the Pantheon and Sant'Ignazio. It is owned by a
very nice couple; the wife hostesses and speaks English.
Try *bresaola all'arancia* and *calamari alla griglia*.

Pamela Keech

6.6 A Clerical Shopping Spree

📖 via dei Cestari, a small street running north
from Largo di Torre Argentina to the Pantheon

Unlike the large tourist emporia near the Vatican, the shops
along via dei Cestari cater primarily to the clergy themselves.
After hours of admiring the great monuments of Christian
Rome, I often found it relaxing to come here and observe
its personal side. The young nuns window-shopping (so
like their secular sisters on the Corso) offer an excellent
reminder of the very human individuals who helped build
this great religious capital. For those seeking more tangible
rewards, the stores here offer decidedly unusual souvenirs.
A favorite amongst savvy (if strapped) shoppers are the dis-
tinctively colored cardinal's socks at Ditta Annibale
Gammarelli in via Santa Chiara.

R.J.W. Cro

6.7 Santa Maria Sopra Minerva

Piazza della Minerva

Risen Christ
Michelangelo, 1514–1521

Most persons' least favorite work of Michelangelo. But in
the gloom of the Dominican Church of Rome, this marble
paean to the human body, to classical antiquity, and to
Christian faith speaks eloquently and majestically to those
who will look with patience and love. It is unnerving to see
Christ nude, but it is also fitting and decorous. He has risen
from the dead, his flesh proclaims the triumph of the
Resurrection.

WILLIAM E. WALLACE
Art historian, author, Washington University

RECOMMENDED READING 105

ROME'S LATIN INSCRIPTIONS

ANNO DOMINI MCCCCXXII IN DIE SANCTI ANDREE
CREVIT AQUA TIBERIS USQUE AD SUMITATEM
ISTIUS LAPIDIS TEMPORE DOMINI MARTINI PAPE V
ANNO VI *("In the year of the Lord 1422 on the day of
Saint Andrew [Nov. 30] the water of the Tiber rose as far
as to the top of this stone, in the time of the Pope Martin
V, his sixth year.")*

The oldest of numerous such flood markers on the
exterior wall of Santa Maria Sopra Minerva.

PAUL PASCAL
Classicist, University of Washington

6.8   ## Piazza della Minerva

Moving from the Bernini elephant in one direction one enters
the church of Santa Maria Sopra Minerva, full of treasures,
from the tombs of Saint Catherine of Siena and Fra Angelico
to the glorious Carafa Chapel frescoes of Filippino Lippi; in
another direction one comes to the Pantheon, the best-
preserved Roman temple, Hadrian's architectural masterpiece. Moving in still another direction, one soon reaches
Sant'Ivo, one of Borromini's triumphs, passing en route the

delightful church and campanile of Sant'Eustachio (stopping for the best cappuccino in Rome at the homonymous bar).

HELEN F. NORTH
Classicist, Swarthmore College

Elephant, with obelisk
Bernini, 1667

Pope Alexander VII wanted this monument to glorify his reign, according to Georgina Masson, "as the famous Bernini fountain with the obelisk in Piazza Navona had done that of Innocent X, and he himself composed the inscription on the base, which says that the elephant was chosen to show that it requires a robust intelligence to uphold solid wisdom."

Rome's small piazzas are perfect places to "feel" the city. Beautiful art in intimate public spaces—some surrounded by outdoor restaurants, most filled with parked cars—all beautiful nonetheless.

PETER SCHWEITZER
Journalist

ALSO RECOMMENDED BY
FRANK HOLMES

6.9 ## Ditta M. Poggi
via Pie' di Marmo 39, between Largo Argentina and the Pantheon, ☎ 06 67 93 674, 06 67 84 477

Poggi is the best art supply (and paper) store in Rome, run by a terrific guy named Memmo. He talks passionately about painting and his own collection, which includes some drawings by his favorite, Balthus, the Count Balthassare Klossowski, who shops there for canvas and paint and brushes. Memmo is a wonderful character and if you are going to ask for a *sconto* it will have to come from him. He seems to know all painters living in Rome. Poggi sells excellent prestretched canvases, prepared and gessoed at the store, and you can order your own dimensions.

DENNIS CONGDON

6.10   Statue of the foot / Pie' di Marmo

via Santo Stefano del Cacco

It's surprising to come upon this large piece parked on the
side of the piazza like a car.

PIKE POWERS

Artist, art director

6.11   Enoteca Corsi

via del Gesù 88, between Corso Vittorio and
Piazza della Pigna

Incredibly good, this wine store/trattoria is really a working
folks' café, and a place where you can sit down for a meal
and not pay a lot. Their *tonno e fagioli* is fantastic. It does fill
up by 12:30, so plan to go there around noon.

PAMELA STARR

6.12   Vecchia Locanda

vicolo Sinibaldi 2,   ☎ 06 68 80 2831

The first-time visitor to Rome must eat pasta and some of
the best I've had was at Vecchia Locanda near the Pantheon.
Try the gnocchi al limone con scaglie di parmigiano or the
stringozzi con gorgonzola e radicchio.

ARTHUR LEVERING

6.13   The Pantheon

Hadrian, 125 AD

Come here first, before you go anywhere else, because this
gigantic round temple with a perfect hemispherical dome
is the best-preserved example of ancient Rome's greatest
contribution to art history (and perhaps to civilization)—a
grand, dramatic, imposing, inspiring interior social space.
Even though the original piazza seems a bit submerged
beneath the surrounding Renaissance pavement, and no
longer has the colonnade that provided an entry sequence,
inside the visitor can experience the ancient city as its
builders did. After this, you can imagine the Roman Forum

and Imperial Fora not as a series of ruins, but brimming
with life and enclosed like the modern, medieval, Renaissance,
and Baroque city on higher ground.
Jayne Merkel
Art historian and critic

Regardless of time of year, be it sunny weather or rain, no
matter from what direction one approaches or happens
upon it, there is no other site that so overwhelms, excites,
startles, and amazes.

    At various times and in various lights of day and night it
can seem the very epitome of a house of worship, the grandest theater, a mere market, or a solemn tomb. In the early
morning hours, passing it with a heavy heart, it can easily
be mistaken for a giant human skull sitting for all eternity
like some abandoned Baroque still life. On festival days the
same building can seem as buoyant, as weightless, as jubi-
lant as a balloon.
Jeffery Rudell
American Academy in Rome

In this building, in constant daily use since it was built almost
1900 years ago, you can stand in a spot where its patron, the
emperor Hadrian, stood, as must have so many visitors to
Rome since. Name them—Charlemagne, Napoleon, etc.—
they had to have placed themselves in the center of the
building, just under the oculus.
Kenneth D. S. Lapatin
Classical archaeologist, Boston University

The hemispherical dome implicitly scoops the viewer on the
floor up into its scope. Nowhere else does one feel so firmly
located on the earth, where the earthly and the heavenly
combine—in contrast to elevated Christian domes, which
wrench the heavens from earth.
Jeffrey Schiff
Artist

If it ever is snowing when one is in Rome, head directly and
as quickly as possible to the Pantheon. Seeing a white column of snow drifting down the middle of the Pantheon is a

once-in-a-lifetime experience.

WILLIAM WYER
Rare book seller

Splendid calm space especially in the rain when a column of mist/rain stands under the oculus. The power of this complete geometric interior space is overwhelming and wonderfully memorable. This building provides a door through which we enter the world of Imperial Rome.

THOMAS L. BOSWORTH
Architect, University of Washington

Christmas Eve concerts are memorable.

KIMBERLY ACKERT
Architect

Not only is the Pantheon a great masterpiece of technology and design, it is virtually the only one to survive intact from antiquity, so that the first-time visitor to Rome can experience one of the great accomplishments of Roman architecture as it was meant to be seen. Some imagination is required, of course, to think away the heavy 19th-century *aediculae* of the second story, but in any other of the great monuments like the Baths of Caracalla or the Basilica of Maxentius and Constantine in the Forum, interiors are exposed to the sky and the marble decoration is missing, leaving only the brick skeleton. Seeing the Pantheon first can help a novice visitor reconstruct those other Roman monuments in his or her mind's eye.

SUSAN WOOD
Art historian, Oakland University

Go there in the sunshine and watch the disk of light traverse the interior, like some giant inside-out sundial. Go in the rain and watch a cylinder of raindrops—isolated from the 180-degree vault of sky—fall as if in slow motion to the floor.

WILLIAM E. WALLACE
Art historian, Washington University

After twenty-four years my memory of the grace of Hadrian's Pantheon surpasses that of all other monuments. I believe it is best visited twice. By day, for the magnificent architecture so admired since antiquity. By night, with a glass of Fernet Branca and the light from the Piazza della Rotonda or of the stars. I would beg only that the visitor study before going, or while there, and enjoy thereby. One favorite painting of the Pantheon's interior is by Giovanni Paolo Pannini and can be seen in the National Gallery of Art, Washington, D.C.

JAMES R. TURNER
Landscape architect

Stand inside the portico and watch the rain fall on the piazza from the doorway. From this vantage, it is useful to remember Vitruvius' role as Rome's engineer and his influence on drainage systems. The Pantheon piazza and many others in Rome are not flat. They are uneven places sculpted by rain, run-off, and traffic. Rome is a watershed.

FREDERICK STEINER
Professor of planning and landscape architecture, Arizona State University

A building which has inspired generations of artists, architects, and scholars from the Middle Ages to the present day. All that, and the tomb of Raphael to boot.

BRUCE BOUCHER
Art historian, University College, London

To stand under the oculus on a chill, wet pavement while open to gray scudding light is a privilege, a clammy glory I would seek again even with older bones.

JOHN PECK
Jungian analyst, poet

Most knee-weakening singular architectural space—the birthplace of would-be architects.

PETER KOMMERS
Architect and painter, Montana State University

I especially love the curve of the floor and the oculus. When it rains there is a wonderful sense of inside and outside united. I've been on the roof, back in the 1970s when

you could still get a *permesso*. The vertiginous experience
of leaning over the lip of the oculus is amazing.

JAMES H. S. McGREGOR
Professor of comparative literature, University of Georgia

It may seem obvious, but as the ancient answer to the
medieval Piazza Navona and the Renaissance St. Peter's, it
is the space that best summarizes the Roman contribution
to architecture: it is an interior that encompasses the world.
Developed to enclose a perfect sphere, it brings heaven to
earth, or earth to heaven. The oculus gives views of passing
clouds and the circle of the sun on the wall. If you are lucky
enough to be there when it rains—the column of water
falling into the center of the room is true magic.

ROBERT McCARTER
Architect, University of Florida

Herodotus tells us that the Persians, when they made an
important decision sober, reconsidered the matter when
drunk (and vice versa) and would carry out a measure only
when they came to the same decision in both states. In the
periods of time I have spent in Rome, I feel the same about
the Pantheon, that a decision should be made inside that
marvelous building, and away from it. Even with hordes of
tourists, one feels a tremendous sense of calm when one is
inside. Architecturally the Pantheon has no peer, and it is
staggering that Michelangelo planned the vault of St. Peter's
to be not an inch wider than the Pantheon (for he knew that
a vault that wide would not collapse). Every church in Rome
owes its integrity to the architects and engineers of the
Pantheon.

STEVEN LOWENSTAM
Classicist, University of Oregon

One of the most beautifully defined spaces I have been in.
As in a Vermeer painting, light itself defines everything in
this enormous structure. The *Meditations* of Marcus Aurelius
reflect the philosophical and spiritual underpinnings of
this building.

ANNA BLUME
Teacher and writer

The Pantheon embodies the Roman architectural genius
for sculpting monumental space. No visitor to Rome should
ignore an opportunity to experience this building, which
proved so influential to later Western architecture. An historical note: the Pantheon also played an important part
in the Christianization of the urban landscape. In 609 it
became the first pagan temple to be converted into a
Christian church. Later legends embellished the temple's
transformation, attributing the hole in its roof (the oculus)
to the hasty departure of expelled demons.

R.J.W. CRO
Archaeologist and art historian, Princeton University

The perfect demonstration of the manner in which Roman
architects combined poured concrete with the vault to create the first architecture of interior space.

JOHN KENFIELD
Archaeologist and art historian, Rutgers University

The original building on this site was built by Marcus Agrippa
in 27 BC. The inscription on the *trabeation* records the
inscription from the earlier temple and is the reason it
traditionally had been dated incorrectly. Excavation in the
19th century proved that most of the bricks of the foundation
are stamped with a date corresponding to 125 AD, placing its
construction in the reign of Hadrian. The building was
abandoned for centuries and was only saved because it was
given by the emperor Focas to Pope Boniface IV, who turned
it into a church in 609. The gilt bronze covering of the roof
was removed in 663 and, in 1625, Urban VIII (the Barberini
pope) removed the rest of the bronze from the beams of the
portico to make eighty cannons for Castel Sant'Angelo and
the four spiral columns of Bernini's Baldacchino in Saint
Peter's. From this comes the witty Roman saying *"Quod non
fecerunt barbari, fecerunt Barberini"* ("Whatever the barbarians didn't do, the Barberini did"). Curiously enough, it
seems that when the tomb of Vittorio Emanuele II was built
inside around the turn of the century, bronze cannons from
Castel Sant'Angelo were melted down for the purpose, thus
"restoring" the bronze, in a strange way, to its original site.

The entrance was originally approached by a staircase,

but the level of the city has risen so much that it is now at street level, robbing it of some of its monumentality, but, at the same time, making it more intimate. There are sixteen monolithic columns forty-two feet high in the portico, eight across the front and two rows of four behind. The colossal bronze doors are original and are the largest to have survived from ancient Rome.

Most of the marble has been looted for other buildings, notably St. Peter's. While this is unfortunate, it reveals the brick structure beneath with its enormous blind arches, which transfer the weight of the dome to eight distinct points and protect the cylinder from cracking. This feature was much studied by Renaissance architects, particularly Brunelleschi for the octagonal dome of Santa Maria del Fiore in Florence. The diameter of the hemisphere dome is exactly equal to the height from the floor (140 feet). The dome was made of poured concrete and tapers from twenty feet thick at the base to five feet thick at the oculus. A negative form was first constructed in wood and the concrete was mixed with travertine in the lower section and then with brick and then pumice toward the oculus to lighten the load at the top. The 30-foot-wide oculus is the only source of light for the interior and leaves the building completely open to the elements. It makes for startling effects on a sunny day. Among the most beautiful experiences I have ever had is to have been standing inside on an overcast winter afternoon watching snow silently settle into a corner.

GEORGE BISACCA
Conservator of paintings, Metropolitan Museum of Art

Stendhal in his *Promenades dans Rome* wrote that he had never met anyone who could remain impassive at the sight of the Pantheon's interior, where its great dome vault creates the sense of the sublime. To be perfectly honest, I am also moved by the temple's exterior, its powerful *pronaos*, or vestibule, with its eight tall and massive granite columns supporting the triangular tympanon; and by its position and the effect that the monument creates in the square itself. The sense of historical continuity and discontinuity, of a "sublime" quotation that illuminates all the text that surrounds it, stirs strong responses that deserve some attention.

Let's begin at the front of the temple. The rectangular shape of the space built by the columns and the triangular form of the tympanon upon them produce a sort of elemental fascination—perhaps a response from our unconscious. As each of us knows by experience, we begin at the age of five to draw houses composed from just these two elemental geometric figures, the rectangle and the triangle. As the psychoanalysts teach us* the rectangle surmounted by a triangle—the form of a prehouse or *urhaus*—constitutes a geometric shape that is the matrix of the possibility, for a child, of mastering space, and representing things in the blank space of the page. In drawing that shape, therefore, and in designing through its support the endless figures of his experience, the child manifests his acquisition of the symbolic, which is connected to his individuality, his paternal influence, and finally, through the emergence of the imaginary and the real, with his psychic sanity. Perhaps the front of the Pantheon exhibits this elemental shape with such a sharpness, power, and absolute simplicity that it produces an enchantment, a fascination. The third elemental geometric figure that combines with the other two as a matrix of the possibility of mastering space is the circle. The Pantheon exhibits this as well, from the outside—the circle that appears as the sun or the trees (in children's drawings) expands around and behind the *pronaos* as a brick construction, in the color of *terra di Siena*.

The viewer is not only fascinated by these elemental shapes, but also by the inscription that runs along the beam of the tympanon for about 78 of its 112 feet and displays 25 letters and some full stops. These square letters are the frieze of the monument, the signs that both tell about it and ornament it.

"Marcus Agrippa, son of Lucius, consul for the third time, built (it)," reads the inscription. How Roman that is, in its tremendous economy and in that short indication of Agrippa's *cursus honorum!*

---

*C. Jeangirard, Will de Graff, *La troisième dimension dans la construction du psychisme*, Eres, 1998.

Historians know that the information given here is technically incorrect, since this inscription appears on the wrong building. These words were engraved on an earlier temple built by Agrippa in 27 BC , but after its destruction, they were reused for the new construction by Hadrian in 120–27 AD. Desire to preserve the memory of the first builder? Taste for the charm and the quality of antiquity? Whatever answer one chooses, this reuse of the inscription already suggests Rome's use of monuments of the past as quotations in a present context. This is nowhere so clear and active as in the case of the Pantheon and its piazza.

The viewer can't help reflecting on the deceptive message of this monumental writing: its powerful square letters that would seem to guarantee forever the solidity of their meaning actually lie about the temple on which they are engraved. These letters say what is truthful and correct, but since they have been put, as a label, upon a wrong monument, they become false. The right monument has disappeared forever. Only its letters were saved! And yet one can't stop looking at those magnificent characters, and admiring the gravity of each of them, their readability, their perfect proportion. Other buildings of various centuries define the piazza: today, some of them accommodate the cafés that spread their tables and *ombrelloni* into the street. The fountain, built by Giacomo Della Porta in the 16th century and transformed by the addition of the obelisk in the 17th century, offers, during hot summer hours, a pleasant relief to tourists—the Romans swarm into the piazza mainly in the evening. The Pantheon is integrated in this diversity of styles and epochs as an old painting in a modern room, as a precious piece in the middle of other more or less dignified pieces.

Becoming integrated in different settings during a long series of centuries has not been a smooth process, but the result of rough and rude attrition. Already in classical Rome this monument superseded another that was destroyed; in the course of its long life, our present Pantheon has lost its forecourt, its lining of stucco, the bronze ceiling of its *pronaos*, the gilt bronze covering the cupola, and so on. Its continuity as a monument of Agrippa has meant continuous adjustment and change.

As a quotation from classical Rome in the piazza, the Pantheon produces a double, contradictory effect. On the one hand it risks appearing as a humiliated fragment of the majestic constructions that manifested the power of the Roman Empire, a relic of that lost grandeur. It intimates terrible decay, a fall indeed, the signs of which are visible on its scarred body, in its degraded appearance, in its broken pieces. And as we look around and measure the immensity of that fall by comparing the imposing monument to some of the modest buildings around it, undecorated by marble, devoted to utilitarian ends, we are gripped by an anguishing sense of the irremedial loss of time, and the life that time contains. One's gaze on what was once a magnificent exterior seeks to extract from these remains the secret of what the Pantheon was, of the context in which it dominated. But this endeavor must fail.

In the evening, when the young Romans come and sit on its large flanks of stone, the Pantheon's distance and uniqueness vanish; it is no longer a fragment and a quotation. It simply tells a longer story than the other buildings, but the same story of change and continuity, of degradation and survival, of loss and restitution. Its magic lies in just that power of giving plural meanings, of producing endless evocations.

And the light, that in the evening gilds the whole basin of the square, makes the rectangle and the triangle of the Pantheon's front look less severe, like a child's drawing.

PIETRO PUCCI
Classicist, Cornell University

ALSO RECOMMENDED BY
BETH VAN HOESEN ADAMS, MARY BETTS ANDERSON, ROSS ANDERSON, LIDIA MATTICCHIO BASTIANICH, JAMES L. BODNAR, RICHARD BRILLIANT, STEVEN BROOKE, GREGORY S. BUCHER, ROBERT CAMPBELL, ALDO CASANOVA, DENNIS CONGDON, JUDY DATER, SIMON DINNERSTEIN, CORNELIA AND LUKAS FOSS, JAMES FOWLE, KENNETH FRAZELLE, KATHERINE GEFFCKEN, KATHRYN GLEASON, CHARLES

Gwathmey, Robert G. Hamilton, Gianne Harper,
Gary R. Hilderbrand, Peter J. Holliday, Marti
Holmer, Hardu Keck, David LaPalombara, Francesca
Santoro L'hoir, Theodore Liebman, Iain Low, David
Marsh, Ann McCoy, Mary Ann Melchert, Danny
Meyer, Henry Mirick, Susan Molesky, Helen Nagy,
Virginia Paquette, Pike Powers, Martin Puryear,
Anton Rajer, Sloan Rankin, Michele Renee Salzman,
Jon Michael Schwarting, H. Alan Shapiro, Susan
Silberberg-Peirce, William O. Smith, Harvey
Sollberger, Pamela Starr, Deborah Stott, June N.
Stubbs and John C. Stubbs, Wayne Taylor, Stanley
Tigerman, John Varriano, Anne Weis, Jean Weisz,
Rebecca West, Emily M. Whiteside, Ann Thomas
Wilkins, David Wilkins, John L. Wong

RECOMMENDED READING 4, 7, 59, 68

6.14 ✗ ## Tazza d'Oro Caffè

via degli Orfarri 84, ☎ 06 67 89 792

Best coffee in Rome—for best price. The smell alone is worth
the visit.
Robert McCarter

Some say this is the best coffee in Rome. Pehaps even better
is their *granita di caffè*, frozen coffee interlaced with layers
of whipped cream.
John Jay Stonehill and Judith Stonehill

Go there to get a *granita di caffè* (especially good on a warm
afternoon) and consume it in the piazza in front of the
Pantheon. The Pantheon and the piazza are beautifully illuminated at night.
James M. Lattis

ALSO RECOMMENDED BY
Geraldine Erman, Thomas Gordon Smith,
Pamela Starr

6.15 Fortunato al Pantheon

 via al Pantheon 55, ☎ 06 67 92 788

The pasta *frutti di mare* is unique. Have it for the appetizer, main course, and dessert.
CHARLES GWATHMEY

ALSO RECOMMENDED BY
STEVEN BROOKE

6.16 Chiesa della Maddalena

façade by Giuseppe Sardi, 1735
Piazza della Maddalena

This building captures the sheer joy and exuberance of Baroque Rome. The façade especially is an inextricable mix of architecture and sculpture, and if "architecture is frozen music" this is the proof—the façade seems to be a three-dimensional expression of the music emanating from the organ loft (one of the finest in the city) behind it.
DAVID MAYERNIK
Architect and fresco painter

RECOMMENDED READING 112

6.17 Giolitti Gelateria

via degli Uffici del Vicario 40, ☎ 06 67 94 206

Just follow the ice cream cones, any evening; definitely try the fruit flavors.
PAMELA STARR

Simply the best gelato in the world.
HELEN F. NORTH

A *capo bianco* sundae at the best ice cream shop in Rome.
JAMES L. BODNAR

ALSO RECOMMENDED BY
KENNETH D. S. LAPATIN, JOHN H. THOW

CAMPO MARZIO

6.18   San Luigi dei Francesi
via Santa Giovanna d'Arco

Saint Matthew cycle
Caravaggio, 1599–1600

In this church are three amazing Caravaggio paintings of the life of Saint Matthew: *Calling of Saint Matthew, Martyrdom of Saint Matthew,* and *Saint Matthew and the Angel.* These paintings are dramatic in their use of color, light, and arrangement of narrative subject matter. Caravaggio is one of the most important painters from the Italian Baroque period, and it is incredible that you can walk into this neighborhood church, plunk a 500-lire coin into a light box, and admire these paintings in quiet (it's a church) and in relative solitude. In this intimate setting, one can even stand very close to the work and marvel at Caravaggio's use of glazes and see how he smoothed away almost all signs of brushwork.
DAVID LAPALOMBARA
Artist, Antioch College

Even if the first-time visitor is not particularly interested nor experienced in the field of painting, the power of these three very large canvasses is very accessible, particularly the *Calling of Saint Matthew* on the left, with its dramatic lighting and clarity of forms. The extended hand of Christ is suffi-ciently similar to that of God reaching out to Adam in the famous Sistine Chapel ceiling scene that, since Caravaggio's first name was Michelangelo, I can speculate that he may have taken some kidding about his name and was conscious of this relationship to the work of his great predecessor. One must have a 500-lire coin for the switch that turns on the lights — if the price has not gone up again. You may want several!
JAMES FOWLE
Art historian, Rhode Island School of Design

How to explain or even describe Caravaggio's Saint Matthew

series? Out of the darkness emerge many mysteries. The flow of action and form from one figure to the next is a cause for wonder. The chair leg which breaks out of the edge of the picture—the space comes to life. Saint Matthew can never again be an abstract distant character—his true humanity is brought forcefully into presence.

Robert McCarter
Architect, University of Florida

For me, these three paintings are all about direct revelation and the very human side of saints so important to a Catholicism which wants to appeal to and strike the most general public—very moving images.

Anna Blume
Teacher and writer

ALSO RECOMMENDED BY
Kimberly Ackert, Richard I. Frank, Katherine Geffcken, Gary R. Hilderbrand, J. Richard Judson, James M. Lattis, John C. Leavey, Thomas Oboe Lee, Lydia Lenaghan, Steven Lowenstam, Theodore K. Rabb, Leslie Rainer, Jon Michael Schwarting, Harvey Sollberger, John H. Thow

RECOMMENDED READING 24, 28, 42, 110

6.19 Sant'Agostino
Piazza di Sant'Agostino

Madonna of Loreto / Madonna dei Pellegrini
Caravaggio, 1604–1605

This painting still hangs in an active church, exploiting the original lighting conditions and fully in keeping with a church whose votive offerings range from the 16th century to yesterday. A painting of supreme virtuosity with its statuesque Madonna (based on ancient sculpture as well as observation from life) and its humble, grubby pilgrims. The Virgin stands on the threshold of her house, a symbol of the Church as welcoming home. And a spectacular, truly patriarchal Raphael *Isaiah* just behind you, from 1514 or so, a

A Library Stroll

A tour which requires some *permessi* or
calls for appointments (but not always) is
to visit some of Rome's old libraries. Top
on my list would be the Borromini-designed
Vallicelliana Library at the Oratorio near
the Chiesa Nuova. The Biblioteca Angelica
near Chiesa di Sant'Agostino is good,
and the Archivi at Sant'Ivo just wonderful. There is also the reading room at
the Collegio Romano, across the piazza
from the entrance to the Galleria Doria
Pamphili. It's no longer in use but still
has all its furniture and decoration. If
it is closed to the public, you might be
admitted to the wonderful Biblioteca
Casanatense, founded in 1698. It's a collection of documents relating to church
history that includes many old manuscripts,
scrolls, and incunabula. Even going to the
old American Library (Centro Studi
Americano) is a pleasure. It's on the via
Caetani (on the way, look for the plaque
marking the place where Aldo Moro's
body was found). The Palazzo Caetani,
through which you have to wend your way
to find the library, is reward enough.
MARY ANN MELCHERT
American Academy in Rome,
1984–1988

RECOMMENDED READING 102

ITINERARY

a Biblioteca Vallicelliana
(in the Oratorio di
San Filippo Neri)
Piazza della Chiesa
Nuova 18,
☎ 06 68 826 071

b Biblioteca Angelica,
Piazza di
Sant'Agostino 8,
☎ 06 68 75 874

c Archivio di Stato di
Roma (at Palazzo
della Sapienza), Corso
Rinascimento 40,
☎ 06 68 75 324

d Collegio Romano
reading room in
Piazza Collegio
Romana,
☎ 06 67 90 733

e Biblioteca
Casanatense, via
Sant'Ignazio 52,
☎ 06 67 98 855

f Centro Studi
Americano (in Palazzo
Caetani), via M.
Caetani 32,
☎ 06 68 80 1613

time when Jews gained respect from Sant'Agostino's great theologian, Egidio da Viterbo.

INGRID D. ROWLAND
Historian, University of Chicago

Compare Caravaggio's *Madonna dei Pellegrini* and Raphael's *Isaia Profeta* and see what can happen in art in ninety years.

JAMES L. BODNAR
Architect

An extraordinary demonstration of this artist's ability to conceive old subjects in new ways.

DEBORAH STOTT
Art historian, University of Texas–Dallas

ALSO RECOMMENDED BY
JON MICHAEL SCHWARTING, ANN THOMAS WILKINS

RECOMMENDED READING 80

Madonna del Parto
Jacopo Sansovino, 1516–1521

Still the object of a cult with scores of folkloric testimonials on adjacent walls. The sculptural group must be one of the few works of "High Art" that still functions as a religious icon.

BRUCE BOUCHER
Art historian, University College, London

RECOMMENDED READING 9

 Osteria del Orso

 via dei Soldati 25, ☎ 06 68 64 250

At dinner, all you can eat of divine Roman antipasto. The waiters bring out plate after plate and leave them on your table. Prix fixe is about $15 per person. I guarantee this course will make more than a meal.

PAMELA STARR

ALSO RECOMMENDED BY
RICHARD FRANK

6.21 Museo Nazionale Romano in Palazzo Altemps
Piazza di Sant'Apollinare 8, ☎ 06 68 37 59

Magnificent permanent exhibition of ancient Roman and
Greek sculpture near the Piazza Navona. This is sculpture in
a particularly beautiful setting.
PHILIP GRAUSMAN
Sculptor and drawing teacher, Yale School of Architecture

A sensitive and artful renovation of the cardinal's palace.
Beautiful courtyard, perfect-size galleries that display early
Roman sculpture exquisitely.
CHARLES GWATHMEY
Architect

ALSO RECOMMENDED BY
CATHERINE SPOTSWOOD GIBBES, JOHN KEARNEY,
NANCY A. WINTER

Ludovisi Gaul
*Artist unknown, original, c. 230 BC; extant copy,
probably 1st century BC*

Not only is this statue one of the finest surviving works of
Hellenistic sculpture at its most dramatically bombastic,
but it has been inaccessible for far too long. Like most of
the Terme Museum collection, and all of the Ludovisi-
Boncompagni component of that collection, it spent about
twenty years nailed into a crate in a dusty basement after
the decision was made that it was no longer safe to display
antiquities in the old Baths of Diocletian. Therefore,
although this statue was a staple of the art history courses I
had taken since my undergraduate days, I didn't actually see
it until 1994. Visiting the Palazzo Altemps, of course, also
gets you into a beautiful old medieval-to-Renaissance
building, and allows you to see the other great treasures of
the Ludovisi-Boncompagni collection, like the colossal head
of the Deified Livia commonly known as *Juno Ludovisi*.
SUSAN WOOD
Art historian, Oakland University

ALSO RECOMMENDED BY
John Kenfield

Ludovisi throne

Greek, 5th century BC

The Ludovisi throne is not Roman of course but an exquisitely beautiful rendering of Venus/Aphrodite rising from
the sea with attendants and wonderfully graceful (sexy!) girl
musicians on side reliefs.

Elaine Fantham
Classicist, Princeton University

ALSO RECOMMENDED BY
Rudolf Arnheim, Caren Canier

RECOMMENDED READING 34

6.22   ## Sundial of Augustus

10–9 BC
via Campo Marzio 48
*The site can only be visited by special permission,
arranged with the German Archeological Institute*
☎ 06 48 17 812 *or* 48 17 817

In this building near Palazzo Montecitorio you can look
down into a hole where excavators found the marble pavement into which the markings of Augustus' amazing sundial
(a monumental celebration of himself) had been cut. Very
cool, though you need a diagram and explanation of the
whole Augustan premise to make sense of it.

William Turpin
Classicist, Swarthmore College

Augustus' enormous sundial was built in the Campo Marzio
area, between what is today the Piazza di San Lorenzo in
Lucina and the Piazza del Parlamento. Inaugurated in 10–9
BC, it was positioned in obvious relation with the ancient
site of Augustus' Altar of Peace, the Ara Pacis (now in Piazza
Augusto Imperatore). The *Horologium Augusti* consisted of a
vast pavement of white travertine inlaid with huge bronze letters and lines indicating hours, days, months, and seasons. It

was meant to be both a clock and calendar, but its malfunctioning (recorded by Pliny the Elder) led the emperor Domitian to make repairs a century later.

In 1979–1980, German archeologists excavated a small section of the sundial under the house along via di Campo Marzio 48. A plan of the excavated part is visible on the façade of the bar next door. The obelisk that was used as the pointer of the sundial was discovered in 1748 under the house at Piazza del Parliamento 3, and re-erected in front of the Italian parliament on Piazza di Montecitorio. A general overview of the topography of the area can be seen on a panel in the Church of San Lorenzo in Lucina.

JAN GADEYNE
Archeologist, Temple University Rome Program

ALSO RECOMMENDED BY
MARY ANN MELCHERT

PIAZZA NAVONA AND VICINITY

6.23 **Piazza Navona**

The absence of cars and buses allows this to remain the most "people-active" piazza in Rome. One can participate in routine and/or festival activities and view one of Bernini's finest works (the fountain) and the Baroque façade of Sant'Agnese in Agone by Borromini. As one sips coffee at an outdoor cafe, there is the discovery of the success of "theatrical city spaces"—places that cheer the eye, satisfy the senses, and replenish the soul.

EMILY M. WHITESIDE
Consultant on the arts, preservation, and design

Piazza Navona is a composite work of art, reaching from antiquity to the 17th century. One of the great Roman piazzas, originally a stadium created by theEmperor Domitian; in the Middle Ages and Renaissance, a marketplace; redeveloped in the 17th century by Pope Innocent X Pamphili, who commissioned Bernini to create his Fountain of the Four Rivers as its centerpiece in 1651. Innocent also commissioned

the Church of Sant'Agnese from Girolamo and Carlo Rainaldi (1652), which was completed by Borromini (1653–1657), and the Palazzo Pamphili designed by G. Rainaldi, with stupendous gallery frescoes by Pietro da Cortona (1651–1654).
MALCOLM CAMPBELL
Art historian, University of Pennsylvania

OK, so there are throngs of tourists, tacky painters whipping up street scenes for the uninitiated, and some less-than spectacular restaurants. Your best bet is Tre Scalini (see p. 130), which has been in operation since 1882, or just drink here and have a nice light meal at L'Insalata Ricca (see p. 150) on the nearby Largo dei Chiavari. But where else can you sit within view of a Bernini fountain, a Borromini church, and meandering lovers? Despite the frenzied scene, natives haunt the place too. The paper-clip shape of the piazza dates from the 1st century AD when the emperor Domitian built a stadium here.
JAYNE MERKEL
Art historian and critic

This is the best of all the piazzas in Rome, containing extraordinary Baroque works by Borromini and Bernini. It simmers with life, day and night. A space with architectural coherence and a dimension that enables it to be both intimate and monumental.
RICHARD MEIER
Architect

Unequaled as a public space anywhere.
GARY R. HILDERBRAND
Landscape architect

Like so much of Rome, this is a palimpsest of ancient and more modern: the stadium of Domitian, remodeled by the Pamphili family, with fountains by Bernini and a church in part by Borromini. The Café Tre Scalini is a good vantage point for observing the Roman scene.
BRUCE BOUCHER
Art historian, University College, London

AN IDEAL ROMAN AFTERNOON

1. Buy any one of the terrific "Art History Mysteries"
by Iain Pears. (They all feature General Bottando of the
Italian National Art Theft Squad, his lovely assistant
Flavia, and the chaotic but brilliant English art scholar
Jonathan Argyll. They have titles like *The Bernini Bust*,
The Titian Committee and *Giotto's Hand*. *Death and
Restoration* is particularly good, but they're all steeped
in Rome.)
2. Sit in the Piazza Navona and order a cappuccino.
3. Read the book.
NICHOLAS HYTNER
Film and theater director

RECOMMENDED READING 72, 73, 74, 75, 76, 77

Although this is a number one tourist site, it is so vast that
it cannot be corrupted entirely by too many tourists. The
façade of Borromini's Church of Sant'Agnese looms above
the west side, but Bernini's fountain is the principal:
Nile, Danube, Ganges, and Plate—with respective symbolic
beasts—and lots of water when it is working well. Painters
and graphic artists sell their wares at stands, and there is a
massive market in December for items having to do with
Christmas—including marvelous crêche figures. Go to
Piazza Navona any time, day or night.
JAMES FOWLE
Art historian, retired, Rhode Island School of Design

Go at Christmas time, to buy *presepio* (crêche) figures.
FRANCESCA SANTORO L'HOIR
Classicist

RECOMMENDED READING 17, 52, 60, 81

Four Rivers Fountain / Fontana dei Fiumi
Bernini, 1651

Bernini is all over Rome like a spirit.
JAMES R. TURNER
Landscape architect

Bernini again, this time in his generous public mode. This
sculpture makes the square, focuses the capsule space on
the spectacular theatrical effects— water sparkling and
flowing amidst dramatic mythic representation of rivers.
The sculpture commands the architectural scale of the piazza,
yet gives the individual a fully populated microcosm to
explore—altogether makes one of the great public ambiances
in the world.
JEFFREY SCHIFF
Artist

One must bask in the spray and beauty of this exquisite
fountain, especially if it's one of those days when the sun
pulses just so across the water.
DAVID ST. JOHN
Poet, University of Southern California

Bernini's sculpted figures turn their collective backs on
Borromini's church.
STANLEY TIGERMAN
Architect

One of many striking Roman "presentations" of water, masterly, affecting, and memorable not just in themselves, but in their settings.

HARVEY SOLLBERGER
Composer, conductor, Music Director of the La Jolla Symphony Orchestra

Theater, spectacle, and the articulation of public space—elements of both totalitarian and entrepreneurial-capitalist urban architecture in our time—can be appreciated better, in all their panache and menace, if one sees either Bernini's Piazza di San Pietro or this fountain. Leo X said that it added ten years to his life; what it might do for one of us is unpredictable, but can only help clarify our sense of where we have come from.

JOHN PECK
Jungian analyst, poet

ALSO RECOMMENDED BY
ELAINE FANTHAM, GILBERT FRANKLIN, PETER J. HOLLIDAY, ROGER B. MARTIN, EUGENE (GENE) E. MATTHEWS, DANNY MEYER

RECOMMENDED READING 82, 96, 104

6.24 Toy Stores

Al Sogno (Piazza Navona 53) is fun just to look around in. The Berté store (Piazza Navona 3) is the place to go for dolls by Lenci, at more reasonable prices. They'll ship, too.
FRANCESCA SANTORO L'HOIR

6.25 Bar Tre Scalini

Piazza Navona 28–32, ☎ 06 68 01 996

This bar/gelateria/trattoria is expensive but still fabulous. Have espresso, cappuccino, an aperitif, or a *tartufo* (depending on time of day and your mood).
MALCOLM CAMPBELL

ALSO RECOMMENDED BY
CAREN CANIER, JOHN C. LEAVEY, DEBORAH STOTT

6.26 ROOFTOP BAR-RESTAURANT OF HOTEL RAPHAEL

Largo Febo 2, ☎ 06 68 28 31

VIEW

The fully furnished living-roomlike rooftop bar-restaurant of the Hotel Raphael near the Piazza Navona is the most spectacular perch for a sunset drink. You can see the backs of the campanili of Sant'Agnese in Piazza Navona, a glimpse of the Tiber, and the old Roman ghetto. You are looking over the roof of Santa Maria della Pace, and it is heaven. Dress well, as the Raphael is popular with Italian senators from the nearby Palazzo Madama, and is not a pensione.

WENDY MOONAN
Journalist

6.27 Santa Maria della Pace

Bramante, 1504; Pietro da Cortona, 1656
vicolo del Arco della Pace 5

By day, a fascinating, unfinished Baroque piazza, one of the few attempts in Rome to make an entire piazza a unified work of art. But behind the undulating Baroque façades— and church façade (all by Pietro da Cortona)—is the most astonishing surprise: an elegantly quiet, exquisitely perfect Renaissance cloister by Bramante. If you've overdosed on the Roman Baroque, try this cloister to calm you down. At night, the little square in front of Santa Maria turns into young hipsterville, the sleepy daytime café is packed and jumping, and of course everyone's dressed in black.

BARRY LEWIS
Architectural historian

6.28 Santa Maria dell'Anima

via della Pace 20

Rome has its 17th- and 18th-century face, but there are some clusters of work by High Renaissance masters in close proximity to one another. Bramante's courtyard at Santa Maria della Pace is a perfect 16th-century gem of classical and simple elegance. Inside the church itself is an altar frescoed with Raphael's sibyls, similar to one of those on the ceiling of the Sistine Chapel, which were painted ten years or so earlier by Michelangelo. Raphael's fresco here is freshly restored. In the second chapel there is a carved altar by Antonio da Sangallo the Younger.

Back outside the door, just three steps away is the rear entrance to another Renaissance church, Santa Maria dell'Anima. This is the church of the German community in Rome, and there is a tidiness to it that is unusual for the city. Buried here is Pope Adrian, the last non-Italian pope before the present John Paul. In the 1520s, he tried to pull Rome away from its venal and extravagant ways, but died while he was at it. The Romans gave his doctor a laurel wreath and the city is a triumphant monument to his failure to make it more austere.

Santa Maria dell'Anima's sober façade is by Sangallo the Younger. There is a bell tower by Bramante and three portals by Jacopo Sansovino. In a city of curving and undulating Baroque façades of many colors, here is a fine grey Renaissance face.
VINCENT BUONANNO
Book collector

ALSO RECOMMENDED BY
MALCOLM CAMPBELL, GEORGE E. HARTMAN,
ROBERT LIVESEY, BARBARA STAUFFACHER SOLOMON

6.29 Caffè della Pace

 via della Pace 3, ☎ 06 68 61 216

The Baroque backdrop interplays with café life to transform the city into live theater.
IAIN LOW

It is (or was) the coolest small café/bar. The scene spills out
into the street. Late night, a couple of drinks, the incredible
urban space of the small piazza designed by Pietro da
Cortona, the hip crowd—the boundaries of inside/outside,
old/new, sacred/profane blur, all within twenty feet of
Raphael's fresco of the sybils. Go there from the airport for
an in-your-face arrival to Roma; say hi to Bob de Niro.
Ross Anderson

6.30 ## Antiquario di Giorgio Nisti
Piazzetta San Simeone 26/27,   ☎ 06 68 79 694

Charming.
Anton Rajer

6.31 ## Oratorio dei Filippini
façade by Borromini, 1637–1640
Piazza della Chiesa Nuova

Visit Borromini's interiors here, as well as the façade.
Pablo Conrad
Writer and editor

RECOMMENDED READING 20

6.32 ## Chiesa Nuova
Piazza della Chiesa Nuova

The painting of *The Presentation of the Virgin in the Temple* by
Federico Barocci in the Baroque Church of the Oratorians
was so moving that Saint Philip Neri used to levitate (that's
not the word they used) when praying in front of it. Don't
miss Borromini's clock tower around the corner.
William Turpin
Classicist, Swarthmore College

Seasonal Concerts and Events

WALK THE CITY, scanning the sidewalk posters for the wonderful occasional events—concerts in the ruins and villas, special boat rides on the Tiber, tours of sites that are normally closed, free concerts in the evening at Castel Sant'Angelo. Watch for exhibitions and lectures at the British, French, Spanish, German, or Swiss counterparts of the American Academy in Rome. Also check the "Trovaroma" weekly entertainment guide published in *La Repubblica* every Thursday.

KATHRYN GLEASON
Landscape archaeologist, Cornell University

IF YOU ARE LUCKY ENOUGH to be in Rome during the winter season, October through May, there is a wealth of good concerts and other musical events to enjoy. These include: the Santa Cecilia Orchestra series, tickets available at via della Conciliazione 2, a few blocks east of St. Peter's; the Teatro del Opera; the concerts of early music at the Gonfalone (a former church on the street of the same name); and various visiting international stars whose concerts will be copiously advertised on billboards citywide.

PAMELA STARR
Music historian, University of Nebraska

CHAMBER MUSIC PERFORMANCES are held in the Oratorio di Santa Lucia del Gonfalone (via del Gonfalone 32A, ☎ 06 68 75 952), a lovely room on the Tiber near Ponte Mazzini, with its simple wood benches and rectangular proportions. The ear delights in this rich acoustical space which is so different from the modern concert hall.

WALTER CHATHAM
Architect

6.33 Sant'Ivo alla Sapienza

Borromini, 1642–1660
Corso del Rinascimento 40

One of the most gloriously spiritual rooms in all of Rome;
sublime, soft white light; uncapturable in photographs,
must be personally experienced.
David Piscuskas
Architect

Borromini was like Bernini's "shadow"—contemporaneous
with him but slowly productive while Bernini was prolific;
doing only architecture while Bernini was a painter, scenic
designer, sculptor as well as architect, working on a small scale
while Bernini was grandiose. Sant'Ivo is a jewel of mystery,
introspection, and enfoldment.
Harvey Sollberger
*Composer, conductor, Music Director of the La Jolla
Symphony Orchestra*

The seeming simplicity of this beautiful white interior space
illuminated from the lantern above is a joy to experience.
The geometry of its star-shaped plan is revealed by its structure and evokes a passion for the art of architecture, as only
great works like this one can.
Richard Meier
Architect

So many reasons to see this: the ins and outs of its undulating surfaces, the pure whiteness of its interior, the tactile
sense of its sculpted surfaces, its moldings, its strange curves.
The way it forces your glance upward in a rush. The way in
which the exterior of the cupola disappears in a flash of flame.
The doorway to the exterior that announces "Jurisprudentia"
is a sculpted rebus: one panel has a law book and a balance
(*jus*) the other a snake looking at itself in a mirror (*pruden-
tia*). Look at the snake reflection toothily smiling back—all
sculpted in travertine.
Ingrid D. Rowland
Historian, University of Chicago

Note the fantastic, whimsical spiral lantern and the neighboring tiled roofs on the equally whimsical and exciting square of Sant'Eustachio.

Philip Pearlstein
Painter

The white and spartan cupola is a departure from other Baroque pieces which are usually highly ornate and decorated. Use of light and form rather than surface seems very modern for its era.

Kimberly Ackert
Architect

It's an intensely Baroque structure with very sculptural interior volumes. The spare white spaces clearly show Borromini's energetic formal inventiveness, held in tension by his rigorous geometry.

Martin Puryear
Sculptor

Not a popular icon, and not open all the time, but my favorite building in Rome. Austere materials combine with incredible mastery of space and geometry in the dome.

Robert Campbell
Architect and writer, Pulitzer Prize for criticism (1996)

PAINTED WINDOWS

If you have seen and done it all and have a bit of time to rove, find Piazza Orologio and walk behind the piazza through any of the streets. Keep looking up at the windows and see if you can find the ones which are painted to look like windows. There are numerous painted shutters (*trompe l'oeil*) and one in particular has a *putto* peeking out. Get lost and discover it yourself.

Sloan Rankin
Artist

Although the major view of the exterior from the courtyard
of the Piazza della Sapienza is available almost all the time
and has the special benefit that Borromini knew the building would be regarded from this courtyard (and that means
all parts of the courtyard), the interior of the building is less
readily accessible. The plan of the church is a "star hexagon"
and the sequence of shapes, recessions, and projections as
one looks upward from the floor of the church is so rich that
it cannot be well grasped in a visit or two. I want to know it,
to be able to remember it—which I cannot yet do. The various relationships are subtle and multiple. That was one of
Borromini's gifts. The spire? Dairy Queen!

JAMES FOWLE
Art historian, retired, Rhode Island School of Design

The notoriously difficult Borromini solved the dilemma of
creating a central church. The goal was to create a round
building to embody the ideal of the Renaissance—man and
God both sharing the center. The problem was where to put
the priest, who, if placed in the center, would have his back
to half the congregation. Using a clever geometry based on a
six-pointed star (which had the added political advantage of
representing his patron's family seal), Borromini created a
round room that had a directional axis and thereby a fit
place for the priest.

There is a marvelous secret to this building: Sant'Ivo itself
is an addition to a much older building—Giacomo Della Porta's
Palazzo alla Sapienza, built in 1557 to house the papal university. La Sapienza consists of two parallel structures, each
with a long colonnade, facing each other across an open
courtyard. Borromini's little church sits at the end of the
courtyard like a plug between the two colonnaded buildings.
Traditional Western churches are all made up of the same
three basic elements: the nave, the large space where the
congregation sits; the aisles, the thin columnar walkways
flanking the nave; and the altar, the area at the end of the
nave where the clergy preaches. Borromini's masterpiece,
part renovation, part new structure, part inside, part outside,
is in fact a typical church composition made up of all these
pieces. The outdoor courtyard in the middle is the nave, the

older flanking buildings with their colonnades are the aisles, and the new church itself the altar. Every visit to this wonderful building reveals another remarkable experience.
ROBERT KAHN
Architect

The only prayer is "Let it be open."
JOHN GUARE
Playwright

ALSO RECOMMENDED BY
BETH VAN HOESEN ADAMS, ANNA BLUME, DENNIS CONGDON, JOSEPH CONNORS, GERALDINE ERMAN, BARBARA GOLDSMITH, THOMAS OBOE LEE, THEODORE LIEBMAN, MELISSA MEYER, DEBORAH STOTT, JEAN WEISZ

RECOMMENDED READING 6, 37, 64, 101, 112

6.34 **Bar Sant'Eustachio**

✕ Piazza Sant'Eustachio 82, ☎ 06 65 61 309

Really great *granita di caffè*, fun to hang around to watch *carabinieri* and parliamentarians.
D. B. MIDDLETON

It's the world's best cappuccino. What makes it the best? Ask them. They won't tell you their secret, so just savor, and enjoy…then order another one. Return at least once a day.
PETER SCHWEITZER

For those of us fanatic about our coffee, Sant'Eustachio—unprepossessing in scale and appearance—is the mecca. Notice that the espresso machines have a metal wing attached so that you can't see the *barista* actually make the coffee. This has led to the suspicion that they add some magic elixir to the coffee. Not true—but it sure tastes like it. Having a Sant'Eustachio espresso or cappuccino cup on your shelf at home is, to the hard core, the ultimate status symbol!
ROBERT P. BERGMAN

ALSO RECOMMENDED BY
TIBOR KALMAN, FRANCESCA SANTORO L'HOIR

6.35 Camilloni di Sant'Eustachio

Piazza Sant'Eustachio 54

Two of the city's most famous caffè bars are Tazza d'Oro and Bar Sant'Eustachio, but save yourself the tourist lines: the most superior caffè I've ever tasted was at Camilloni, near Sant'Eustachio. The rich, nearly blue-black chocolate dolci are unforgettable.

KENNETH FRAZELLE

6.36 Sant'Andrea della Valle

Corso Vittorio Emanuele

Frescoes of Sant'Andrea
Mattia Preti, 1650–1651
Apse of Sant'Andrea della Valle

In a city where painting and architecture are consumately linked, these frescoes are perfect examples of the Roman sense of scale—against the overwhelming power of the church nave, these well-over-life-size figures confidently hold their own.

DAVID MAYERNIK
Architect and fresco painter

6.37 Palazzo Massimo alle Colonne

Baldassare Peruzzi, 1532–1536
Corso Vittorio Emanuele 141

As Georgina Masson suggests, if you're in Rome in March, do not miss the day masses are held to commemorate a miracle of San Filippo Neri at the Palazzo Massimo alle Colonne. And don't fail to go around to the back of the Palazzo (via della Posta Vecchia) where the walls have faded frescoes and the colonna stands.

MARY ANN MELCHERT
American Academy in Rome, 1984–1988

Through Tosca's Rome

For any opera fan Rome is, above all, Tosca's city. The
ghosts of characters who never lived haunt the venues
of Rome, from the Castel Sant'Angelo to the basilica of
Sant'Andrea della Valle, to the remote fastness of the
Farnese Palace (now the French embassy and far less
accessible than it was when Scarpia held court there).
Following are some itineraries drawn from hints in the
opera, in the Sardou play on which Puccini's opera was
based, and from a historian's acquaintance with what the
city was like when the events of the opera take place (June
17–18, 1800).

*Cesare Angelotti escapes from the Castel Sant'Angelo and
makes his way to his sister's family chapel at the basilica of Sant'Andrea della Valle.*

Start on the upper levels of the Castel Sant'Angelo, at the
cells reserved for political prisoners. Slip out under the
cover of a party of workmen (tourists will do in a pinch).
Make your way across the Bridge of the Angel and continue along the via Santo Spirito (avoid the Corso Vittorio
Emanuele II as far as possible; it wasn't created until after
1870). Turn onto the via dei Banchi Nuovi and make your
way past the Piazza del Orologio; cross behind the Chiesa
Nuova along the via Governo Vecchio, to the little Piazza
del Pasquino behind the Braschi Palace (site of the Museo
di Roma). Then continue to the corner of the Piazza Navona
and follow the via della Cucagna, then take a sharp left
until you reach the Piazzale Sant'Andrea della Valle. There
you will see the unmistakable façade of Tosca's church.
Inside Sant'Andrea della Valle there is no Attavanti chapel
(where Angelotti takes refuge), but the first chapel on your
left, the Barberini chapel, conceals in its streetside wall a
shallow little chamber separated from the chapel proper by
an ironwork grille. If your sister has hidden a key for you,

you may slip into this little shrine to Saint Sebastian. Otherwise, content yourself with admiring the stunning church, familiar from so many stage productions of the opera, and look for a likely site for Cavaradossi's painting.

Mario Cavaradossi goes from his home on the Piazza di Spagna to Sant'Andrea della Valle; from there to the Ghetto (to buy a bolt of cloth); after he meets with Angelotti both men hurry from the church to a villa on the outskirts of the city.

Sardou tells us that the Palazzo Cavaradossi is located on the Piazza di Spagna, at the foot of the Spanish Steps. To follow Mario to work, walk down the via Condotti, turn left onto the Corso, and go until you reach the via Caravita (opposite the Palazzo Sciarra), where you turn right. Pass the church of Sant'Ignazio, continue along the via del Seminario to the Pantheon, then bear left, back into the tangle of streets to the Piazzale Sant'Andrea della Valle, from which you can see the basilica of Sant'Andrea.

For Cavaradossi's side trip to the Ghetto, leave the church by the side door and turn left onto the via dei Chiavari. Cross behind the church and bear left on via Giubbonari until you cross via Arenula. Once across, via dei Falegnami will take you to the heart of the ancient Ghetto. At the Piazza Mattei, site of the famous turtle fountain, turn right, onto via della Reginella, the only street remaining from the original Ghetto.

Mario and Tosca's villa is located just inside the walls, near the entrance to the most famous of the ancient Roman roads, the Appian Way. You'll want to take a bus or a taxi to the Baths of Caracalla. At Piazzale Numa Pompilio, turn onto via Porta San Sebastiano. Just to the left of the church of San Cesario is the house of Cardinal Bessarione, a Renaissance retreat open to the public which contains a

➤

number of appropriate hiding places for escaped political prisoners.

Floria Tosca goes either from her apartments (perhaps at the Palazzo Venezia) or from rehearsal at the Teatro Argentina to meet her lover at the church of Sant'Andrea della Valle. From there, tricked by Scarpia, she leads the police to the villa, then returns to the city to sing for the Queen at the Farnese Palace.

Tosca, Sardou tells us, is from Verona and thus is a citizen of the Venetian Republic, so she could have apartments at the Palazzo Venezia. You can approximate her walk by leaving from the back of the Palazzo Venezia on via San Marco and walking toward the river on via delle Botteghe Oscure past the Piazza dei Calcarari to the Largo Argentina where the theater is located. Leaving the theater, walk along the narrow via Sudario to Sant'Andrea. Before entering the church, make your way to the Campo dei Fiori (see Scarpia's walk, below). Buy an extravagant bundle of flowers, then retrace your steps to the side entrance of Sant'Andrea, listening all the while for the rustle of clothing as someone slips into the Barberini chapel.

The Baron Vitellio Scarpia goes from his apartments at the Farnese Palace to the Castel Sant'Angelo, where he interrogates the jailer implicated in Angelotti's escape; then, armed with the knowledge that the escapee is hiding at Sant'Andrea, the Baron hurries to intercept him. He fails, but sets his spies to follow Tosca, then returns to the Farnese to await the result of the hunt.

Scarpia's apartments would be on the *piano nobile* (second floor to Americans) of the Farnese Palace. If he left by the back gate of the palace, a gallop along via Giulia (a long, straight street that parallels the Tiber) would bring him to the Piazza Sant'Angelo. There the Bridge of the Angel leads directly to the sally gate of the Castel Sant'Angelo.

To get from Castel Sant'Angelo to Sant'Andrea, Scarpia would more or less duplicate Angelotti's earlier trip (see above) though of course with a great deal less caution.

After the Te Deum, Spoletta and the *sbirri* ("the cops") follow Tosca to the suburban villa (see above). Scarpia, if he feels like a walk, could leave the side door of the church, turn left on via dei Chiavari, a quick right onto the via del Paradiso, then the next left would bring him to the Campo dei Fiori. Brushing aside the vendors, follow him across to the via della Corda (yes, named for the torture device that once stood here), to the Piazza Farnese.

The frantic activity of Act I has set the venues for the remainder of the opera, which takes place at Scarpia's apartments and on the parapet of Castel Sant'Angelo. Get yourself a libretto, plug your earphones into a CD of *Tosca* (the Callas-Di Stefano-Gobbi version is the classic), and enjoy.

SUSAN VANDIVER NICASSIO
*Interdisciplinary historian, University of
Southwestern Louisiana*

The Tosca strolls were adapted from the author's *Tosca's Rome: The Play and the Opera in Historical Perspective*, University of Chicago Press, 1999, and from *The Opera Lovers' Guide to Rome*, ARN Press, 1999.

Buses

AVOID THE #64 BUS unless you've left your wallet at home or put your money in your sock.
MATTHEW GELLER
Artist

THE #64 IS THE BUS THAT SHUTTLES between the Stazione Termini and St. Peter's. It goes along the Via del Corso and Corso Vittorio, two important and popular arteries that run near important sites like the Piazza Venezia and the prime shopping areas. So it is a must for tourists, and an even bigger must for pickpockets. When on this always-crowded bus, anchor your purses under your arm, keep wallets in front pockets under supervision, and in general be extremely vigilant and even paranoid. They are out to get you on the 64 (despite the presence of many nuns), and you need to be perpetually alert.
PAMELA STARR
Music historian, University of Nebraska

WHERE CAN ROME BE EXPERIENCED, BE FELT?
It has to be the buses. Rome is a bus city. Pick an entertainment (the opera, dinner above the Spanish Steps, the Sunday morning flea market at Porta Portese) then get there and back by bus. If your pockets aren't picked or you don't fall in love with some untouchable Madonna or get hit on by a good, married, Catholic male, you won't have had an authentic morsel of the notorious city. I was told on good authority that neither Freud nor Jung could muster the nerve to board a Roman bus.
JAMES R. TURNER
Landscape Architect

CAMPO DEI FIORI

and

THE GHETTO

7

PONTE
PRINCIPE AMEDEO
SAVOIA AOSTA

PIAZZA
DELL'ORO

V.D.
CONSOLATO

V.D. CIMATORI

LARGO DEI
FIORENTINI

VIC. D. PALLE

CORSO VITTORIO EMANUELE II

VIC. D. ORBITELLI

LUNGOTEVERE D. SANGALLO

VIC.
CEFALO

VIC. D.
SUGAN-
ELLI

VIA DEI BANCHI VECCHI

VIC. SF.
CESA

8

V.D.
BRESCIANI

VIA GIULIA

VIA DEI
GONFALONE

VIC. D. CARCERI VECCHIE

V. D. CELLINI

VIC. DEL
CANTARI

V. LARGA

V. CERRI

VIA DEL PELLEGRINO

VIC. D.
SCIMMIA

7

VIC. D.
MALPASSO

VIC. D. PRIGIONI

V. S.
FILIPPO NERI

VIC. D.
MORETTA

VIA DEI CAPPELLAR

PONTE G. MAZZINI

LARGO
PEROSI

V. DI S. AUREA

VIA DI S. ELIGIO

V. D. BARCHETTA

VIA MONSERRATO

V. D.
MONTORO

Tiber River

LUNGOTEVERE DEI TEBALDI

VIA IN
CATERINA

V. D.
ARMATA

VIC. IN
CAPRETTARI

V. S. GIROLAMO
D. CARITÀ

VIC. DEI FARNESI

11

10

VIC.

PIAZZA
FARNE

6

LUNGOTEVERE GIANICOLENSE

V. DEL MASCHERON

VIC. DEL
POLVER

VIC. D.
ARCH

PIAZZA
S. VINCENZ
PALLOT

LUNGOTEVERE DEI FARNESINA

PONTE SISTO

LUNGOT

8

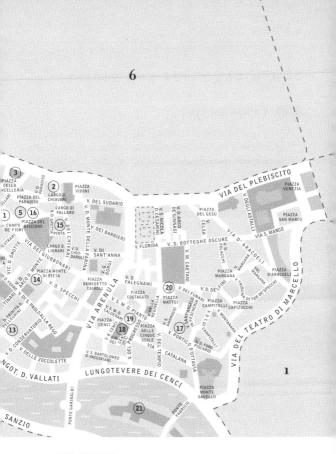

THE GHETTO

N

CAMPO DEI FIORI AND VICINITY

7.1　**Campo dei Fiori**

The most vibrant of Roman squares, where the wonderful street market immediately puts one back in touch with the life and sparkle (and good food) of Rome. Nearby are the Cancelleria and the Palazzo Farnese, the city's finest Renaissance building and its grandest Baroque palace. In the center of the Campo, at the spot where he (like many other victims of the Inquisition) was burned, is a splendid statue of the great and enigmatic philosopher Giordano Bruno.

THEODORE K. RABB
Historian, Princeton University

Wonderful display of produce, from fish in the shady east end to flowers in the sunny west end, and every form of citrus (in season) and a variety of greens most Americans will never have seen. Surrounding shops sell cheeses, meat, and good bread; some adequate restaurants. A center of the kind of urban life that every city would die to achieve.

JAMES H. S. MCGREGOR
Professor of comparative literature, University of Georgia

This piazza has been an important meeting place for Romans and foreigners alike since the 14th century. The *vineria* along the western side serves a quick before-dinner drink (I recommend the sparkling white wine called prosecco) and the flower stalls sell the prettiest stuff in town if you've got a notion to treat your partner to a posey.

KATHARINE BROPHY DUBOIS
Historian

For the first-time traveler to Rome, the outdoor vegetable, fish, and fruit peddler markets are an absolute must. Most lists of such markets would be topped by the one in the Piazza Campo dei Fiori but the guide book could easily list seven or eight. (Our favorite is up in Monteverde Vecchio on via Nicolini.) These are not tourist markets; the people of the city buy food here as they have for a long time. It is a way to see what is in season and a place to be early in the morning. Markets open at first light.

DENNIS CONGDON
Artist, Rhode Island School of Design

SHOPPING AT THE MARKETS

When you buy fruit and vegetables at the market you will see signs designating the price—800 or L.800, for example, scrawled on a little sign over the oranges. What this refers to is the price in lira per *etto*, which is 1/10 of a kilo, a kilo having 1000 grams (there are 450 grams to a pound). Once you make a few purchases, you will be able to judge the relative relationship to the U.S. system. Ultimately the Italian system is easier, as everything is divisible by ten. If you know the amount you wish to buy you can say uno or due, etc., referring to the number of *etti*, but you may also play it by ear by saying *ancora* (meaning more or still), and *basta così* (that's enough!) when the vendor has put enough in the bag.

MARTIE HOLMER
Artist, faculty, Rhode Island School of Design

It's not a glamorous space when empty, but I like the succession of rooms provided by the Campo, the surrounding streets, and the Piazza Farnese and the way the market creates a rhythm in the area that is not immediately discernable if you visit at another time. It's a kind of urban dynamic that one simply cannot reconstruct mentally in even a well-preserved building or site and reveals a cultural/commercial mix that one doesn't find in more traditionally touristic areas.

ANNE WEIS
Art historian, University of Pittsburgh

Go to the market to buy fresh fruit and vegetables for lunch. In the east corner of the Campo is a great salumeria and in the northwest corner a place for bread and pizza bianca or rosa.

ANNA BLUME
Teacher and writer

Mix with one of Rome's most lively neighborhoods—delicately scaled. Not to be missed on New Year's Eve when I did see a couch come hurtling out of one upper-story window, true to the Italian New Year's tradition of ejecting old furniture or appliances to make room for new acquisitions, preferably through an upper-story window.

DAVID PISCUSKAS
Architect

ALSO RECOMMENDED BY
KIMBERLY ACKERT, BETH VAN HOESEN ADAMS, JANIS BELL, SIMON DINNERSTEIN, ALAN FELTUS, CORNELIA AND LUKAS FOSS, BARBARA GOLDSMITH, MARTIE HOLMER, TIBOR KALMAN, SUSAN KLEINBERG, LYDIA AND JOHN LENAGHAN, THEODORE LIEBMAN, ROGER B. MARTIN, EUGENE (GENE) E. MATTHEWS, ANN MCCOY, LESLIE RAINER, MICHELE RENEE SALZMAN, SUSAN SILBERBERG-PEIRCE, ROGER ULRICH, JOHN VARRIANO, JOHN L. WONG

RECOMMENDED READING 47

7.2 **L'Insalata Ricca**

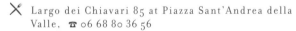

Largo dei Chiavari 85 at Piazza Sant'Andrea della Valle, ☎ 06 68 80 36 56

RECOMMENDED BY
JAYNE MERKEL

7.3 **Museo Barraco**

Corso Vittorio Emanuele 166, ☎ 06 68 80 68 48

The Museo Barraco contains rare early Greek pieces of sculpture.

RUDOLF ARNHEIM
Art historian, University of Michigan

NAMES OF ROME

A number of street names in the historic center of Rome recall the congregating in past times of artisans of various specialties: around Campo dei Fiori are the via dei Giubbonari ("makers of coats"), via dei Baullari ("trunk makers"), via dei Chiavari ("locksmiths"), via dei Pettinari ("makers of combs"), vicolo dei Chiodaroli ("nail makers' alley"), via dei Capellari ("wigmakers"), via dei Balestrari ("crossbow makers"), via dei Cartari ("paper makers"), and via di Santa Maria dei Calderari ("Saint Mary of the tinkers").

Nearer to Piazza Navona, on the other side of the Corso Vittorio Emanuele, you'll find the via dei Leutari ("lute makers"), via dei Coronari ("rosary makers"), and via dei Staderari ("makers of scales").

Many of the words in this list are obsolete in contemporary Italian but the street names survive tenaciously and suggest some of the sights—and sounds—of the medieval and Renaissance city.
PAUL PASCAL
Classicist, University of Washington

7.4 Grappolo d'Oro

✗ Piazza della Cancelleria 80, ☎ 06 68 64 118, or 06 68 97 080

RECOMMENDED BY
DEBORAH STOTT

7.5 Pollarolla Ristorante

✗ Piazza dei Pollarolla 24 (Campo dei Fiori), ☎ 06 68 801 654

Great atmosphere, great food, frequented by celebrities (ate

Via Giulia during the Christmas season

If you travel to Rome during the Christmas season, please slow down enough to take a leisurely walk down the via Giulia. The via Giulia is a long, straight street built by Julius II at the beginning of the 16th century. During the Christmas season, decorative lights and piped-in holiday music provide the perfect backdrop for individual Nativity scenes displayed in every storefront window. There must be fifty or more of these crêche displays, so take your time. You can even begin or conclude your *passeggiata* with a nice dinner at the Taverna Giulia (see p. 154). By the end of the evening, you'll agree this was a little bit of magic during a special time of year.

DAVID LAPALOMBARA
Artist, Antioch College

ITINERARY

a via Giulia

b Taverna Giulia,
   Vicolo del'Oro 23

at table next to Marcello Mastroianni once). Great location by Campo dei Fiori.
ALDO CASANOVA

7.6 **Palazzo Farnese**

Antonio da Sangallo, Michelangelo, 1514–1589
Piazza Farnese
Open to the public only one day per week, with admission only by advance appointment, at Cultural Services of the French Embassy, ☎ *06 68 60 11*

The Triumph of Love

Annibale Carracci, 1597–1604

The best alternative to the Sistine ceiling: the Carracci frescoes of the gods at play on the ceiling of the Galleria Carracci—joyous paintings, full of color and amazing *trompe l'oeil.*
ARTHUR LEVERING
Composer

These frescoes of the great lovers of history, including Bacchus and Ariadne, rival the ceiling of the Sistine Chapel in beauty and composition, and they are more accessible to the viewer, once one gains entry to the French embassy.
JUNE N. STUBBS AND JOHN C. STUBBS
Professor of Italian, Virginia Polytechnic Institute and State University; Professor of English, Virginia Polytechnic Institute and State University

ALSO RECOMMENDED BY
DAVID KONSTAN

7.7 **Il Drappo**

✕ vicolo del Malpasso 9, ☎ 06 68 77 365
reservations required

RECOMMENDED BY
DAVID M. MARSH

THE ANTIQUE SHOPS OF VIA GIULIA

If your budget permits, why not take home a little of the
most historic city on earth? Ancient portrait busts are
my fantasy favorites, but the furniture, paintings, and
other wares for sale in the antique shops of the via di
Monserrato off Piazza Farnese and via Giulia are more
enticing than those I've seen, en masse, anywhere. A
stroll through these streets alone is memorable, even to
an anti-shopper. If you succumb to temptation, then are
feeling pinched, cross the Tiber and have dinner in one
of the lively student-filled pizzerias and beer halls in
Trastevere.

JAYNE MERKEL
Art historian and critic

7.8 **Da Luigi**

Piazza Sforza Cesarini 24, ☎ 06 65 45 463,
06 68 65 946

Another comparatively inexpensive trattoria located handily
in a small piazza just opposite the Chiesa Nuova. Gorgeous
pasta specialties; one of my favorites is the penne alla
vodka.

PAMELA STARR

7.9 **Taverna Giulia**

vicolo del Oro 23, near the Ponte Principe
Amedeo, ☎ 06 68 69 768

RECOMMENDED BY
DAVID LAPALOMBARA

7.10 Ar Galletto

Piazza Farnese 102, ☎ 06 68 61 714

Fine old trattoria in the corner of the piazza, with outdoor
tables where you gaze up at the façade of the Palazzo Farnese
as the sun sets and swallows swoop over the rooftops. Less
hectic than its neighbor La Carbonara in Campo dei Fiori.
PABLO CONRAD

7.11 San Girolamo della Carità

via Monserrato 62A, ☎ 06 68 79 786

Cappella Antamoro
Filippo Juvarra, 1708–1710

A beautiful, late Baroque creation, the fruit of a remarkable
collaboration between Juvarra and the sculptor Pierre Legros
the Younger. The chapel conveys a better impression of a
Baroque *bel composto* than any other, particularly through
Juvarra's subtle use of colored light and the (almost) claus-
trophobically small scale on which he worked. The ambience
and the statue of Saint Philip Neri resonate well together.
BRUCE BOUCHER
Author and art historian, University College, London

RECOMMENDED READING 67

7.12 Palazzo Spada

mid-1540s, restored in 1650 by Borromini
Piazza Capo di Ferro 13

Wonderful visual inventions, inside and out.
GERALDINE ERMAN
Artist

Borromini perspective

Ask the guard for permission to view the *perspettivo*. Inside,
turn left and look down through a wide pane of glass set in
the library at the view through a deep colonnaded corridor,
ending in a little courtyard with a large statue in it. If possible,

ROME'S LATIN INSCRIPTIONS

CAESAR DICTATOR: UNIVERSUM TERRARUM ORBEM
HOSTILI CRUORE REPLEVIT, SUO DEMUM SANGUINE
CURIAM INUNDAVIT *("The Dictator Julius Caesar: He
filled the whole world with his enemy's gore, and at the
end he drenched the senate with his own blood.")*

Inscription on a statue of Caesar in the façade of
Palazzo Spada, circa 1560.
PAUL PASCAL
Classicist, University of Washington

get the guard to let you walk into the corridor, to experience
the actual height and distance of the corridor and the tiny
sculpture at the end. The *trompe l'oeil* effect is achieved
through decreasing the size of the columns in the colonnade.
It's worth making an appointment to view it, if necessary.
There are fine paintings in the Galleria Spada collection.
SLOAN RANKIN
Artist

7.13 L'Evangelista

X via delle Zoccolette 11-a (the front entrance)
or Lungotevere Vallati 24 (the back) near the
Monte Pietà, ☎ 06 68 75 810

This wonderful restaurant is a must, for their two specialties:
the *carciofi al mattone* (an artichoke flattened between two
bricks and baked) and *vino prugnolo*, with a subtle aroma of
prunes.
JEFFERY RUDELL

L'Evangelista serves the best cannelloni I've ever tasted.
FRANK STELLA

7.14 ## Chapel of the Monte di Pietà

Piazza del Monte di Pietà 33, ☎ 06 51 72 66 95

While this chapel is often closed because it's owned by a
bank, it is one of the most complete early 18th-century
ecclesiastical spaces in Rome and an aesthetic delight.
MICHAEL CONFORTI
Director, Clark Art Institute, Williamstown MA

7.15 ## The Theater and Porticus of Pompey the Great

62 BC

Located between the Campo dei Fiori and Largo Argentina,
this complex requires a discerning eye, one perhaps already
familiar with the depth of Rome's urban layers. Seen from
the air, the curve of Rome's first stone theater and the
orthogonal layout of the great adjoining quadriportico are
clearly evident in the overlying architecture of the medieval
fabric.(This plan view is available on menus and images
displayed in the restaurants built down into the vaulted
masonry substructures of the theater: Pancrazio's and
Costanza's on the via del Biscione.) The visitor on via dei
Chiavari is on the ancient stage and can look up to see the
theater's *cavea* dramatically expressed in the high curved
façades of the palazzi on the via di Grotta Pinta. Strollers
heading to Largo Argentina along the via del Sudario or via
di Santa Anna are following the same walks as those once
shaded by the monumental porticoes with their fabulous
Greek paintings and columns hung with Pergamene fabrics
of spun gold. The via dei Barbieri is the remnant of the great
axial promenade through the interior park of the Porticus,
a grove of stately plane trees shading fabulous statuary,
both commissioned and gathered from around the Empire.
The abundant fountains were supplied by the Aqua Virgo.
Intended as a great monument to early Imperial victories,
the porticoes are best remembered by the ancient poets as
a favorite rendezvous for lovers on hot August afternoons.
At the end of the axis was a large hall used as a Senate house
or *curia* during spectacles in the theater. Standing at the
balustrade of the sunken archaeological park in Largo

Argentina, just between the Teatro Argentina and the end
of via dei Barbieri, the visitor can look straight down to see
the remains of the back wall of this *curia*, just meters from
where Julius Caesar was assassinated at the feet of the statue
of his rival Pompey (Shakespeare conflates the story—the
body was brought to the Forum Romanum only after the
assassination).

Kathryn Gleason
*Landscape archaeologist, Cornell University, co-principal
investigator of the American Academy in Rome Excavation
at Horace's Villa, Licenza*

7.16 **Da Pancrazio**

Piazza del Biscione 92,   ☎ 06 68 61 1246

Trattoria tipica di quartiere (early 1960s).
Wayne Taylor

The restaurant is in the substructure of the Teatro di Pompeo
where the Roman Senate met because of lack of room in the
Curia in the Forum. It was here Caesar was killed. Great to
eat *paglia e fieno* (hay and straw) and admire the *opus reticu-
latum* (ancient Roman brickwork) on the walls.
Hardu Keck

THE GHETTO

7.17 **Da Giggetto**

via Portico d'Ottavia 21/22,   ☎ 06 68 61 105

There can be few more charming places to dine than the
Trattoria da Giggetto in the heart of Rome's ancient Ghetto.
Founded in 1923 by Luigi Ceccarelli, whose nickname was
"Giggetto," the restaurant specializes in the traditional
dishes of the district: artichokes cooked in olive oil; filet of
cod fried in a batter of flour, water, and yeast; and zucchini
flowers stuffed with mozzarella cheese and slices of anchovy
and fried. Ideally, one should have a meal at Giggetto on a
warm summer evening when tables are set up outside. Just

steps away are the ruins of the Porticus of Octavia, constructed
by Augustus in honor of his sister. Inside the Porticus, a
church, Sant'Angelo in Pescheria—the name commemorates
the fact that the city's fish market was established here in
the 12th century—was constructed in 755. Thus at Giggetto
one dines deliciously surrounded by the astonishing history
of the Eternal City.
David Garrard Lowe

ALSO RECOMMENDED BY
Katharine Brophy Dubois, Marjorie Kreilick,
Ernst Pulgram, Peter G. Rolland, Harvey Sollberger,
Pamela Starr, John H. Thow

7.18   **Da Piperno**

via Monte de' Cenci 9,   ☎ 06 65 42 772,
06 68 80 2772

Some of the best food in Europe.
Stanley Tigerman

Fabulous setting. Wonderful Jewish-Italian cuisine.
Rebecca West

Rome's Latin Inscriptions

Italiae Fines Promovit Bellica Virtus et
Novus in Nostra Funditur Urbe Decor
(*"Warlike valor has advanced the boundaries of Italy,
and new beauty is lavished on our city."*)

Commemorating the first success of Fascist imperi-
alism in Africa, on a 1937 building in the Piazza
Sant'Andrea della Valle. The building itself has not
aged gracefully, an irony whose full force is lost on
those who must bypass the Latin.
Paul Pascal
Classicist, University of Washington

Through the ages

This stroll encompasses Republican, Imperial, medieval, and modern Rome, with a touch of the Baroque and the Renaissance. Walk from Trastevere's Piazza in Piscinula, noting the medieval houses, across the Tiber Island bridges (Ponte Cestio, Ponte Fabricio) to the Ghetto. View the Teatro di Marcello. Along the via del Portico Ottavia, note the tiny church, Sant'Angelo in Pescheria, installed in a corner of the ancient Roman portico. Its name refers to the use of the ruined portico as a fish market, from the 12th century. The inscription on the Casa di Lorenzo Manilio at the end of that street dates it to 1468. Glimpse the Baroque by looking in at the church of Santa Maria in Campitelli. Renaissance Rome appears in the Cenci Palace beyond the end of the Portico Ottavia.

CHARLES WITKE
Classicist, University of Michigan

ITINERARY

a Piazza in Piscinula (Trastevere)

b Ponte Cestio / Ponte Fabricio (Tiber Island)

c Teatro di Marcello, Sant'Angelo in Pescheria, via del Portico d'Ottavia

d Casa di Lorenzo Manilio

e Santa Maria in Campitelli

f Palazzo Cenci

A walk through the Portico d'Ottavia into the Jewish ghetto
is a journey into the layers of Rome. Piperno helps to weave
those layers together.
FREDERICK STEINER

ALSO RECOMMENDED BY
ANNA BLUME, CAREN CANIER, CHARLES GWATHMEY

RECOMMENDED READING 30, 31, 32

7.19 Al Pompiere

via Santa Maria dei Calderari 38, ☎ 06 68 68 377,
06 65 68 377

Wonderful *carciofi alla Giudea* and *fiori fritti* (lightly battered
fried zucchini blossoms). It also has wonderful *secondi* and
pasta and the service is impecccable. It is tucked away on a
quiet street near Largo Argentina off via Arenula.
JANIS BELL

7.20 The Turtle Fountain / Fontana delle Tartarughe

*Taddeo Landini, 1581–1584, from a design by
Giacomo Della Porta*
via dei Funari

The Turtle Fountain always represented to me the serendipity
of an ordinary Rome stroll: to discover a perfect, delicate
fountain of exquisite beauty tucked away in a small courtyard
of an unremarkable street. Unlike, say, the fountains of the
Piazza Navona, this is not a "destination" attraction; it's something you would ideally stumble upon en route to somewhere.
RICHARD ROTH
Journalist

The Turtle Fountain in the Ghetto neighborhood is visually
exciting and unlike any other fountain in Rome. Each of
its life-sized, highly individualized four nude young men
is twisting and springing up to grab turtles from the basin
overhead—or maybe they are tossing the turtles in.
PHILIP PEARLSTEIN
Painter

The bridges of the Tiber

Take a stroll linking the nine bridges on the Tiber, starting with Ponte Sant'Angelo in front of Castel Sant'Angelo and ending with Ponte Sublicio. This walk can give the first-time visitor a wonderful comprehensive tour of Rome, some of her best neighborhoods, and various notable sites near these bridges.

Rocío Rodríguez
Artist and painter

ITINERARY

a Ponte Sant'Angelo

b Ponte Vittorio Emanuele

c Ponte Principe Amedeo Savoia Aosta

d Ponte Mazzini

e Ponte Sisto

f Ponte Garibaldi

g Ponte Cestio/Fabricio

h Ponte Palatino

i Ponte Sublicio

One comes upon the fountain through small streets totally
by surprise; it is indeed a wonderful piece as sculpture and
as a part of a very energetic space. It is surrounded by beautiful old buildings, and is perfect in scale. The design and
modeling are lovely, and though it is almost sentimental, it
is a thoroughly beautiful piece of its kind.

Lawrence Fane
Sculptor

7.21 Tiber Island / Isola Tiberina

Tiber Island's formation and development is shrouded in
Roman myth and legend. In 293 BC it became the site of a
sanctuary to the Greek god of healing, Askleapios (whose
importation to Rome from Epidaurus is related by Ovid).
The island is now dominated by the Hospital of the Fatebene
Fratelli and by the church of San Bartolomeo (within which
is a 12th-century wellhead). Its bridges are ancient—the
Pons Fabricius, from 62 BC, is the oldest surviving bridge in
Rome. You can still see traces of the island's ancient travertine façade decorating it to look like a floating boat, perhaps
in reference to the arrival of the cult of Aesculapius.

Margaret Brucia
Classicist

Look for the remnants of the carved stone ship's prow that
the ancient Romans placed on the down-river end of the
island (I found only a small portion of the carvings depicted
in Piranesi's famous print). To get the best view climb down
the stairs from the present bridge to the river bank.

Philip Pearlstein
Painter

I always take or send people there; they then inevitably end
up exploring the neighborhoods on both banks, which are
real old-Rome in feeling.

William Turpin
Classicist, Swarthmore College

Walking over most of the Tiber bridges brings one to the Ponte Fabricio, with its Janus head(s), which leads to the Ospedale San Bartolomeo and a carving on which one can see the god of healing, Askleapios, represented as a snake winding around a staff. The restaurant at the bridge head is known for delicious roast lamb.

URSULA HEIBGES
Classicist, Middlebury College

ALSO RECOMMENDED BY
JOHN LENAGHAN

RECOMMENDED READING 71

ROME'S LATIN INSCRIPTIONS

CAPITA PISCIUM HOC MARMOREO SCHEMATE LONGITUDINE MAIORUM USQUE AD PRIMUS PINNAS INCLUSIVE CONSERVATORIBUS DANTO (*"The heads of fish longer than the markings on this marble shall be given to the magistrates, up to and including the first fin."*)

Medieval Latin text on the Portico d'Ottavia, near a marble slab from the Roman fish market.
PAUL PASCAL
Classicist, University of Washington

TRASTEVERE

and

THE JANICULUM

8

Map labels:

V. D. MONTE DEL GALLO
V. DEL MONTE DEL GALLO
CLIVO DI MONTE DEL GALLO
V. STAZIONE DI S. PIETRO
V. D. SILVERI
VIA DELLE FORNACI
VIA INNOCENZO III
VIALE VATICANO
VIALE DELLE MURA AURELIE
VIA ALDO FABRIZI
V. D. ORTI D'ALBERTI
V. S. FRANCESCO DI SALES
VIA DELLE MANTELLATE
VIC. S. F. DI SALES
V. S. FRANCESO DI

VIA GREGORIO VII
RAMPA BRANCALEONE
V. D. ARGILLA
V. S. SILVERIO
VIC. D. GELSOVINO
F. BORGONCINI DUCA
PIAZZA
V. A. CERIANI
VIC. D. VICARIO
VIA DELLE FORNACI
PASSEGGIATA DI GIANICOLO
VIA NUOVA D. FORNAC
THE GIANICOLO
VIA DEI R

VIA ROVERELLA
VIA DELLA CAVA AURELIA
VIA S. LUCIO
(17)
PIAZZALE GIUSEPPE GARIBALDI
VIA ALDO FABRI

VIA AURELIA ANTICA
(1)
V. DELTA
S. PANCRA
PIAZZALE AURELIO
V. G. GARIBALDI
(16)

(27)
VILLA DORIA PAMPHILI
VIA D. S. PANCRAZIO
(21)
(23) (22)
(20)
V. A. MASINA
VIA GIACOMO MEDICI
V. DELLE MURA GIANICO
V. CADOLINI
VIA MERCANTINI
V. F. DAVERIO
PIAZZA F. CUCCHI
V. A. ALGARDI
V. F. BONNET
V. F. VASCELLO
VIALE DEI
V. P. ROSELLI
VIALE A. LEDUC
VIA CALANDR

PIAZZA S. PANCRAZIO
V. BASILIO
V. GUAS. TALLA
VIA GIACINTO CARINI
VIA CALANDR

VIA VITELLIA
PIAZZA OTTAVILLA
V. F. BOLOGNESI
V.O. REGNOLI
V. G. DEZZA
VIALE DELLE MURA GIANICO
(24)

V. COSMO DE TORRES
VIA DEI QUATTRO VENTI
V. BUSIRI VICI
V.F.S. SPROVIERI
V. G. ROSSETTI
LENSI
V. U. BASS
VIALE
V. DEI PAMPHILI
VIA INNOCENZO X
VIA FONTEIANA
VIALE DI VILLA PA
VIALE DEI QUATTRO VENTI
V. R. GIOVAGNOLI
PIAZZA ROSOLINO PILO
V. M. QUADRIO
AURELIO S

CLIVO RUTARIO
PIAZZA FONTEIANA
V.L. DI MONREALE
V. S. CALEPODIO
V.A. COLAUTTI
V. F. CAVALLOTTI
V. A. POERIO
V. A. MARIO
VIA CESARI
(26) (25)

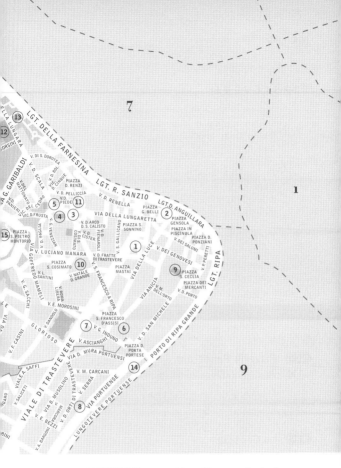

N

TRASTEVERE

...some of Rome's most fascinating medieval churches, hidden in cobbled back streets.

HENRY D. MIRICK
Architect

Funky, "Left Bank" atmosphere of old Rome.

REBECCA WEST
Professor of Italian literature and cinema studies,
University of Chicago

The most interesting neighborhood as a neighborhood; the wonderful small streets and piazzas and churches never become boring.

ROBERT CAMPBELL
Architect, writer, Pulitzer Prize for criticism (1996)

ALSO RECOMMENDED BY
J. RICHARD JUDSON, JOHN KEARNEY

8.1 **Pizzeria Panottoni**

viale Trastevere 53, ☎ 06 58 00 919

Absolutely the best pizza I have ever had.

CELIA E. SCHULTZ

8.2 **La Gensola**

Piazza della Gensola 15, ☎ 06 58 16 312

Excellent Sicilian cooking, expecially seafood. Pasta with sardines, great bowls of steamed shellfish, with the perfect sauce to be soaked up with fresh bread.

THOMAS OBOE LEE

8.3 **Piazza of Santa Maria in Trastevere**

The church is splendid, the fountain has been restored, and the surrounding maze of little streets with down-home

restaurants and shops and wonderful palazzi as well.
DAVID KONSTAN
Classicist, Brown University

The church itself, good dining, bookshops, gelaterie, etc.,
make this general area one of my favorites for an evening
out.
JAMES M. LATTIS
Historian of Astronomy, University of Wisconsin—Madison

8.4 Santa Maria in Trastevere

12th century
Piazza di Santa Maria in Trastevere

This basilica is still a touchstone for me each time I return
to Rome. It is rugged enough and lovely enough to be
absolutely consoling. The mosaics, the kids in front kicking
soccer balls at the grating…what could be better, or more
Roman?
DAVID ST. JOHN
Poet, University of Southern California

The mosaic floor is a deep pleasure; there are many other
experiences of time and beauty in this church.
ANDREA CALLARD
Artist

The endless fascination of Rome lies in its layered character:
those buildings and places in which cultures and periods sit
side by side or have been grafted onto each other. It is the
triumph of variety and continuity—of history and cultural
richness—over aesthetic purity and unity. Few places bring
this so strongly and picturesquely into focus as the Church
of Santa Maria in Trastevere. Located on a piazza of great
beauty (have a coffee, ice cream, or lunch while enjoying
this square, whose character changes with the time of the
day), this basilica—the first we know of to be dedicated to
the Virgin—is a virtual mirror of the layered culture that makes
Rome unique. The tower (campanile) is Romanesque; the
mosaics decorating the upper portion of the façade of the

12th century; the portico by Carlo Fontana built in 1702. The
three doors into the church are reused Roman entablatures
and moldings; inset into the portico walls are ancient and
paleo-Christian inscriptions as well as actual tombs.The
interior of the church (4th century; rebuilt 1130–1140) is
conspicuous for its extraordinary series of Roman columns,
capitals, bases, and pieces of entablatures—all mismatched
and used to confer an effect of Imperial splendor—much
enhanced by the early afternoon sun falling through the
yellow-tinted windows. The inlaid pavement is medieval
cosmatesque (made from fragments of ancient marble,
restored in the 19th century, when the frescoes of the nave
were added). The wonderfully intricate gilt wood ceiling,
with its central painting of the Virgin, was designed by the
great 17th-century classical painter Domenichino, who also
designed the elegant winter choir at the end of the right aisle.
The whole climaxes in the sumptuous raised apse, which is
decorated with 16th-century frescoes and one of the most
splendid and important medieval mosaics in Rome: above is
Christ, the Madonna, and saints (c. 1140); below are extraordinary scenes of the life of the Virgin and an image of the
Madonna and Child adored by the donor (c. 1291). The latter
are among the very rare works by Pietro Cavallini—together
with Giotto and Duccio a founder of Italian painting.
Cavallini's art is directly indebted to his own work as a
restorer of now-lost early Christian fresco cycles and with
him the whole effort at the recovery of the visual language
of antiquity gets underway. The charm of these scenes will
quickly give way to admiration for narrative concision.
(Cavallini's greatest surviving fresco cycle is in the nun's
choir of Santa Cecilia in Trastevere—a ten-minute walk from
Santa Maria—and can be viewed on certain mornings: check
at the church). In the left aisle there is also a delightful
Baroque chapel by Antonio Gherardi (1680) with an amus-
ing cupola.

KEITH CHRISTIANSEN
Curator of Italian paintings, Metropolitan Museum of Art

ALSO RECOMMENDED BY
WILLIAM TURPIN

Mosaics of the Life of Mary
Pietro Cavallini, 12th century

The detail and realism provide a direct link between the
present and the past. Santa Maria in Trastevere is a wonderful medieval refuge from the dominant Baroque elsewhere
in the city.

FREDERICK STEINER
*Professor of planning and landscape architecture, Arizona
State University*

8.5 La Tana di Noantri, Hostaria-Pizzeria
via della Paglia 1-2-3, ☎ 06 58 06 404

A best and most reliable traditional Roman trattoria within
easy access of the American Academy. A favorite of Academy
Fellows and locals of Trastevere—discovered but not quite
"ruined" by the tourists. Recommended are the artichokes
and penne *arrabiate* as well as the antipasto table at the
door.

BENJAMIN KOHL

An unassuming restaurant in a spectacular location, especially when weather allows outside dining. Very wide choice
of *casalinga* (home-style) dishes. Location permits visit of
the church and the piazza.

ELFRIEDE AND GEORG KNAUER

Tucked just behind Santa Maria in Trastevere, this trattoria
has tables in the garden area across the street. A leisurely
pranzo can take most of the afternoon. Begin with Frascati,
the white wine from the nearby Castelli Romani. Then *gnocchi alla Romana* (baked semolina gnocchi, a dish that can
be traced back to Imperial Rome; Apicus gives a recipe for this).
Abbacchio (grilled baby lamb). A *misticanza* (a salad of mixed
wild and domestic greens). And *macedonia di frutta* for
dessert.

JOHN JAY STONEHILL AND JUDITH STONEHILL

8.6   San Francesco a Ripa

Piazza San Francesco d'Assisi 88

Albertoni Chapel

The height of Baroque experience, and not overly frequented by tourists. Notice the remarkable thickening of the chapel wall which requires prolonged visitation in order to experience the interplay of architecture and art through the medium of light.

IAIN LOW
Architect

Beata Ludovica Albertoni

Bernini, 1674
Albertoni Chapel

This work, so seldom seen by tourists, still has the ability to surprise—just as Bernini intended. The agony/ecstasy of Ludovica's death and heavenly reception are experienced.

DAVID G. WILKINS
Historian of art and architecture, University of Pittsburgh

This is a more intimate, and perhaps therefore more moving, variation on Bernini's more famous monument to Saint Theresa. Here, in a consummate integration of painting, sculpture, architecture, and light, is a perfect example of his idea of the *bel composto*, or beautiful whole, which inspired so much of Rome's Baroque art and architecture.

DAVID MAYERNIK
Architect and fresco painter

ALSO RECOMMENDED BY
DAVID KONSTAN, THOMAS OBOE LEE, PIETRO PUCCI,
DEBORAH STOTT, CRAIG H. WALTON, NANCY A. WINTER

RECOMMENDED READING 41, 113

Cell of Saint Francis

Amazing room-size reliquary (ask for permission to view).
GERALDINE ERMAN
Artist

8.7 Casa della Gioventù

Luigi Moretti, 1932
via G. Induno and viale Trastevere

The former headquarters of the Fascist youth organization Gioventù Italiana del Littorio in Trastevere is another example of modern work by Luigi Moretti (he designed the Palestra di Scherma, see p. 236); it introduces plasticity in both concept and form. The tower faces the Tiber and is best viewed from the Aventine directly across the river. Moretti's work for the Fascists displayed a particular latitude given the stylistic criteria imposed by the regime and his Casa della Gioventù employs subtle effects to strengthen its political-aesthetic argument. Only the tower's main door and the ubiquitous balcony compromise its front plane. Emphatically, this element is the face of the building, replacing a more conventional concept of façade in an Elementarist composition. It organizes and represents the complex ensemble behind it. While it appears as a simple flat marble shaft topped by a flange, close inspection reveals that the tower has a slightly curved edge, converging as it nears the top; it's a pilaster, or a sectioned column, and the flange is a capital. As if to accentuate the typically Fascist historicist-progressivist alloy, here Moretti contrasted a glazed corner stairwell, of impeccable Bauhaus purity, to the eccentric entry column. Inside the main building there is a cinema and offices.

MICHAEL STANTON
Architect

8.8 Columbaria at the Museum Drugstore

via Portuense 303

The goofy Museum Drugstore is a combination supermarket-bar-disco and used car dealership, which houses a group of very well-preserved and tended columbaria. This innovative method of preserving archaeolgical remains—building around them instead of burying them—is an experiment of Fiorenzo Cattali of Soprintendenza Archeologico.

FRANCESCA SANTORO L'HOIR
Classicist

8.9 ## Santa Cecilia in Trastevere
Piazza di Santa Cecilia

Statue of Santa Cecilia
Stefano Maderno, 1599

I love the story of Santa Cecilia, who sang her way through
two botched attempts at execution for practicing Christianity
to become the patron saint of music. Her body was exhumed
in 1599 and found "not lying upon the back, like a body in a
tomb, but upon the right side, like a virgin in her bed, with
her knees drawn together, and offering the appearance of
sleep." Maderno was called in to make a statue of her unusual
pose. His inscription says, "Behold the body of the most holy
virgin Cecilia, whom I myself saw lying incorrupt in her tomb.
I have in this marble expressed for thee the same saint in
the very same posture of body."
PAMELA KEECH
Sculptor, installation artist, historian

ALSO RECOMMENDED BY
WILLIAM TURPIN

STROLL

Through Trastevere on via della Lungaretta

The via della Lungaretta offers an easy introduction to
my favorite part of the city, Trastevere. Although it seems
almost an alley by contemporary standards, this street
was an important artery in the medieval city. A stroll
along its length brings one past some of the area's most
important monuments, as well as numerous small piazzas
and side streets. The latter beg to be explored, as they
offer rare glimpses into the texture of medieval Rome
(in addition to some of Trastevere's best restaurants).

R.J.W. CRO
Art historian and archaeologist, Princeton University

8.10 Torre da Ficino

X via di Natale Grande off the Piazza San Cosimato
closed Monday

Order a whole pizza, which serves one nicely. It's thin-crusted,
and loaded with sumptuous toppings such as artichokes,
mushrooms, sausage, or anchovies. (Remember, pizzerias
open at 7:00 p.m, whereas most regular restaurants only
open at 8:00.)
PAMELA STARR

8.11 Cinema Pasquino

vicolo del Piede 19,   ☎ 06 58 03 622

The ceiling rolls open during the evening movies at this
English-language cinema (not dubbed).
PIKE POWERS
Artist, art director

8.12 Galleria Nazionale d'Arte Antica in Palazzo Corsini

via della Lungara 10,   ☎ 06 68 80 23 23

Venus Discovering the Dead Body of Adonis
Jusepe de Ribera, 1508–1511

She is about to alight: her bare, milk-white foot still floats
above the dark brown earth at the bottom of the painting.
Above it are fluttering draperies, billowy clouds, white doves,
and, at the very top, her flushed face crowned with roses and
framed by golden hair. Twisted trees, the same deep brown
as the earth, stretch bare limbs toward her as if intent on
stopping her. We follow her anxious, fixed gaze across the
space of the painting, all the way down, to the very opposite
corner: there, surrounded by a blood-red drapery and muddy
earth, we see the deathly pale body of her lover.

She is Venus, goddess of love and also of nature, gardens,
and flowers; he is Adonis, a shepherd whose beauty won her
love. Recklessly, Adonis hunted a boar who gored and killed
him with his tusks. Venus heard his cries and flew to him,

but was too late. Ribera's painting shows the awful moment of her discovery. Her face is not yet filled with despair: she is expectant, perhaps relieved to have found him at last, perhaps not yet aware that he has already died. We sense impending gloom not in her rosy face, but in the dark, swirling shapes around it. The sky seethes with movement. Venus' arms stretch out, reaching stark silhouettes of trees and dark underbellies of clouds. As we look at the painted surface, our eyes refuse to rest but glide along seamless paths, from drapery, to cloud, to tree branch, and back again to outstretched arm, bent neck, and shoulder. Adonis himself is caught up in this sweeping movement. His arms describe a graceful spiral around his face; his receding legs lead our eyes toward, and almost seem to touch, Venus' still-floating bare foot; his body curves sharply downward, its outline a perfect mirror of the tree above, whose trunk reaches up towards Venus' hand. All these staged connections and dancelike twists and turns seem strangely gay and full of life, at odds with the painting's somber colors. We are inclined not to believe the deathly pallor of Adonis's skin: we suspect he is not quite beyond all hope.

Indeed, Adonis does come back to life. According to legend, Venus' grief at her lover's death was so great that she would not allow the lifeless body to be taken from her arms. Eventually, the gods consoled her by decreeing that Adonis might live again for half of each year—spring and summer— while Venus might spend the other half—fall and winter—with him in the lower world of the dead. Ever since, Venus leaves this earth each year: her absence is felt by nature in fall and winter, while each springtime her return from the underworld makes flowers bloom and gardens grow.

SANDA ILIESCU
Artist, designer

8.13 **Villa Farnesina**

Baldassare Peruzzi, 1508–1511
via della Lungara 230
Open mornings only

The Farnesina was the first suburban villa of the 1500s. One must imagine the villa standing alone on the banks of the Tiber with no other buildings surrounding it. It was, and is, outside the wall of Rome on the Trastevere side of the Tiber River. (What distinguishes a villa from a palazzo is that the first is suburban or outside the city, while the palazzo is urban and within the city.)

Artistically, the Farnesina is one of the most original pieces of architecture and painting in Rome. The building's design is ingenious in its siting and its relationship to its garden and to the river. The façade facing Rome is stripped down save the elaborate cornice abounding with cherubs dancing between candelabra. This façade pretends to be urban because it has the more austere character of a city palazzo, whereas the spectacular garden façade, or party façade, is a giant, five-bay, arched and open loggia. Architecturally the loggia links the building to the outdoor space. To further enhance this link, the loggia itself, painted by Raphael and his assistants (1517 through 1518), simulates a garden pergola or arbor.

Equally original in form and content is the river loggia, which is unconventionally placed by Peruzzi at a right angle to the garden loggia. The loggia openings have been filled in with windows and no longer retain the original form. However, the loggia was intended to open up to the Tiber and again to be a link between the building and the outdoor space or the river. This loggia was never frescoed as Raphael intended, save one panel or bay. Its theme was to be water, versus the garden/foliage theme of the garden loggia. The single panel that exists from Raphael's scheme is his famous *Galatea* (1511) or nereid (female sea creature). She, sensuous and beautiful in her pose, is being drawn by dolphins on a seashell. Galatea is surrounded by cherubs and tritons (male sea creatures).

If this is not enough for one building, go upstairs and discover Peruzzi's Sala delle Prospettive, a total illusion. The room exemplifies Peruzzi's art, which integrated architecture and perspective. The walls of the room are painted to simulate the inside of an elevated temple. The artist wanted his client, Agostino Chigi, and his guests to feel as if they were elevated on a plinth in a temple looking through simulated marble columns toward the city of Rome on the one hand, and toward the countryside through the columns on the opposite wall.

In short the Villa Farnesina is a multipurpose spectacle which can give a first-time visitor so much artistically and all in one place. It is also a very peaceful precinct to retreat to from the splendid chaos that is Rome.

JUDITH DiMAIO
Architect, Yale University

To see a Renaissance painting without the crushing crowds of the Vatican, visit the Villa Farnesina frescoes by Giulio Romano and other students of Raphael, as well as a painting of the Graces by the master himself. In another room, *trompe l'oeil* views of Rome painted by Peruzzi (the architect of the villa) were also executed in the the early 1500s.

VINCENT BUONANNO
Book collector

Loggia of Cupid and Psyche
Raphael, 1510-1519

There are works that epitomize an artist's career. Others that transform our understanding of him or her. Every art history student has an image of Raphael as the painter of serene images of the Madonna and Child or of those grandiose frescoes—among them the *Disputa* or the *School of Athens*—in the Vatican. But how many think of Raphael as the inventor of Baroque illusionism—of frescoes that make the observer an active participant? His work for the Sienese banker Agostino Chigi does just that and creates a springlike ambience inspired by Apuleius' *The Golden Ass*. This is one of the high-water marks of Renaissance art. On the vault of what was an open loggia (now glazed) designed by the great Sienese architect Baldassare Peruzzi, Raphael designed scenes from the story of Cupid and his beloved Psyche, who, after various tasks, is finally admitted to the company of the gods. The paintings are by Raphael and his pupils, including Giulio Romano.

The ceiling is conceived as though the images are two enormous tapestries suspended on lush arbors garlanded with fruit and vegetables to shield the viewer from the sun. The spandrels frame figures against the sky—as though hovering above our heads. The pagan joy and wit of these scenes no less than their sheer beauty provide endless delight. (Fortunately, there are chairs to make the viewing more pleasurable.) The scene of Jupiter and Cupid provided the germ for Caravaggio's *Inspiration of Saint Matthew* (a rejected version of the one in San Luigi dei Francesi, which was destroyed in World War II), and the whole scheme was the basis of Annibale Carracci's decorations in the Palazzo Farnese—usually considered the first great Baroque fresco cycle in Rome. Botanists: bring along your field glasses to study the extraordinary fruits and vegetables, painted by a specialist in Raphael's shop, Giovanni da Udine. And don't miss the phallic cucumber fertilizing a fig above the hand of Mercury—just in case you didn't get the erotic subtext of the story!

Incidentally, in the adjacent room is Raphael's celebrated fresco of Galatea with a companion scene of Polyphemus painted by Sebastiano del Piombo; also astrological frescoes by Baldasssare Peruzzi. The upstairs room with fictive architecture by Peruzzi and a bedroom with frescoes by Sodoma are not bad either. This is the most pleasurable way to acquaint yourself with the world of the Renaissance.

KEITH CHRISTIANSEN
Curator of Italian Paintings, Metropolitan Museum of Art

ALSO RECOMMENDED BY
HARDU KECK

Galatea
Raphael, 1511

The Villa Farnesina is one of Rome's hidden treasures. Begun in 1510 by the banker Agostino Chigi from designs by Baldassare Peruzzi, the villa was conceived as a suburban retreat near the Tiber. "Agostino the Magnificent," as he was called, made his villa a monument to the splendid humanism of the Renaissance. The villa was decorated by Sebastiano del Piombo, Sodoma, Peruzzi, and, most spectacularly of all, by Raphael. In the Sala di Galatea his glorious fresco of Galatea, the statue brought to life by Aphrodite after its sculptor, Pygmalion, falls in love with it, is dazzling. This is one of the most classical in style of all Raphael's paintings. There is no fusion here of figure and atmosphere, but an almost bas-relief effect that harkens back to the Hellenistic-Roman world. The blue sky with its white clouds, which forms the picture's background, resembles marble, while the sea below is still. In the villa's high, vaulted rooms and in the exquisite surrounding gardens, Agostino Chigi received the leading artists and poets of the age, as well as princes and cardinals and the Pope himself. Here philosophy and astrology were discussed, poetry recited, plays performed, and new music presented. Lucullian banquets were served upon dishes of silver and gold. All this lives only in legend, but on the wall of the Sala di Galatea is Chigi's greatest and most enduring monument, Raphael's painting, elegant and so alive that the viewer would not be too surprised if Galatea, in her rich, red cloak, stepped into the room.

DAVID GARRARD LOWE
Art historian, author

RECOMMENDED READING 12, 25

8.14 **Porta Portese**

Via Portuense and other streets between Piazza Porta Portese and Piazza Ippolito Nievo
Sunday only

Largest flea market in Europe—people as diverse and interesting as the stuff and both range from the unbelievably common to surprisingly refined.

GEORGE E. HARTMAN
Architect

One can find an enormous array of international junk.

PIKE POWERS
Artist, art director

Lots of entertaining stuff—stores, antiques, clothes. At the main entrance turn left for the old guys with the funny junk and fake antiques and great cheap seconds of Italian dinner-

ware. Turn right for clothes and new stuff and frames and
big antiques. Bargain. Go early. There are pickpockets.
VIRGINIA PAQUETTE AND WILLIAM O. SMITH
Artist; Composer, University of Washington

One can spend wonderful hours looking for treasures and
experiencing the people. Walking through Trastevere in the
back streets is the real view of old Rome. There is nothing
like it elsewhere in the city. Go early.
LYNN KEARNEY
Artist, curator

Old objects and new, some by Abruzzi craftsmen.
RICHARD FRANK
Classicist, historian, University of California–Irvine

It is now twenty-eight years since I last spent a Sunday morning at Porta Portese. Will all my merchant friends recognize
me; will I still be a young man? I'm sure it will be just the
same and Bruno the Abruzzi bedspread salesman would
invite me for a coffee and comment on my latest purchases.
THEODORE LIEBMAN
Architect

ALSO RECOMMENDED BY
JENNY STRAUSS CLAY, JUDY DATER, GERALDINE ERMAN,
JOHN C. LEAVEY

THE JANICULUM

8.15 ## San Pietro in Montorio
Piazza San Pietro in Montorio 2, just off via
Garibaldi

Tempietto
Bramante, 1502

This little High Renaissance gem demonstrates how the city
of Rome has drawn on its own past for inspiration over time
as it reinvented itself and the history of architecture at the

absolutely highest level. This perfectly proportioned, little, free-standing, circular chapel was inspired by the wonderful 1st-century round temples of ancient Rome, which themselves derive from primitive huts and Greek *tholos*, as well as by later domed structures like the Pantheon, but its exterior elevation was as carefully considered (if not more so) as its interior form. It is nestled beside the Quattrocento church of San Pietro in Montorio with a Baroque chapel by Bernini (second from left), a moving *Flagellation* by Sebastiano del Piombo (1518), and, outside, a breathtaking view of old Rome.

JAYNE MERKEL
Art historian and critic

It is a tiny temple perfectly expressing the Renaissance ideal of architectural symmetry.

JOHN JAY STONEHILL, *Architect*, AND JUDITH STONEHILL

It tells me about scale of buildings. It is, in fact, a piece of sculpture in a courtyard. After seeing the Tempietto, I'd stop at the Aqua Paola fountain and contemplate the world.

THEODORE LIEBMAN
Architect

ALSO RECOMMENDED BY
JENNY STRAUSS CLAY, SIMON DINNERSTEIN,
PETER KOMMERS

8.16 **Fontana Paola**

altered by Carlo Fontana, 1690
via Garibaldi

...to throw coins (Trevi is for tourists!).
FRANCESCA SANTORO L'HOIR
Classicist

ALSO RECOMMENDED BY
KENNETH FRAZELLE, LYDIA LENAGHAN, HELEN NAGY

Sebastiano's Rome

In a letter attempting to explain his difficulties with a
commissioned altarpiece, Rubens complained of a "*perversi
lumi.*" Bad light pervades the churches of Rome, yet
sometimes it can be more of a blessing than a curse.
Discovering a great painting all by oneself is a thrill that is
hard to come by nowadays. Usually, the great paintings are
thrown at us, overpresented and overlit, but a few are still
somewhat hidden in their original settings, awaiting discovery. What light there is in these Roman churches has
been mismanaged over the centuries, diminished by care-
less renovations. Not surprisingly, the Church of San
Pietro in Montorio, just such a dark case, made for a perfect discovery. Pushing my son's stroller over a worn stone
floor, I looked up into a reveal to catch a poorly defined
aura, the afterglow of what had to be a special painting.

A late-winter afternoon in Rome is not the best time
to stalk 16th-century church painting. It's very hard to
find your prey. But that afternoon I did flush a great painting out of the Janiculum's shadow. I had no idea of its
source. It looked like a Renaissance painting, but it easily
could have been a copy, like the compositionally striking
Caravaggio I had seen a few days before at the Palazzo
Corsini, a fantastic *Narcissus*, easily the highlight of the
collection. I had been very disappointed when my wife
read the label of the *Narcissus* to me—a "copy after
Caravaggio." I went into a deep sulk, wondering why I
couldn't tell an original from a copy and why this copy
was so good, because even confronted by its lack of authen-
ticity, I still wanted it. To me it was a hot painting from
the moment I saw it, maybe the hottest cool painting I
had ever seen.

The painting in San Pietro in Montorio didn't have the
boxy modernism of the *Narcissus*, but it did have a special
kind of in-your-face classicism. It was an over-the-altar

➤

painting with mural power, one with "a tiger in its tank." My first guess was a conservative one, maybe after Giulio Romano; my second guess was, "I just don't know." I was surprised by the attribution to Sebastiano del Piombo, but not by the title, *The Flagellation*; the darkness was not so great that I couldn't make out the action.

Three months later I was there, again late in the afternoon, when the painting was perfectly lit, the seasonal angle of the the sun being now in my favor. Sebastiano's painting was beautiful, inventive, and expansive. The beauty was all Sebastiano's, brought out by his Venetian gift for full-scale color, intensely articulated and swirling across the canvas from side to side and from top to bottom. Beauty brought out also by his paint-handling and form-building skills, so evident that Michelangelo, in Sidney Freedberg's words, had no reservations about selecting Sebastiano as his deputy in what amounted to a Medici-driven painting contest with Raphael.

The inventiveness in the painting owes something to Michelangelo's design, which allowed Sebastiano to run wild with a full-blown painterly classicism tinged opportunely with an innate piety. Painterly, pietistic classicism may sound strange, perhaps even at odds with itself, but it is a quality that really counted for a lot in the following hundred years of painting.

Finally, *The Flagellation* has a convincing expansiveness, an ability to make narrative action and gesture fill the pictorial boundaries to the point that they seem to swell and and bow out the framing edges. In a similar way, Sebastiano's work pushes painting itself beyond the confines of the 16th century into the 17th century. It is clear, too, that it was Sebastiano's brand of Roman painterly classicism that helped make the expansion so fluid and so far-reaching. He easily caught the attention of Caravaggio and Rubens, as we can see by their magnificent versions of the Flagellation. Certainly, this power-enhanced 16th-century Roman art had no trouble beaming itself out

➤

all over Italy and across Europe, led, for example, by Sebastiano's *Flagellation* to Naples and Antwerp. And it's equally certain that any painter, having seen the Roman light, *perversi lumi* as it could often be, was bound to follow its path all over Italy, and all across Europe, as the history of Western painting so clearly attests.

FRANK STELLA
Artist

8.17 **Piazzale Garibaldi**

A good visit, especially with children, is to watch the noon cannon being fired just below the Piazzale Garibaldi. One should arrive by 11:45.

ANN HARTMAN
Artist

The masterful Garibaldi monument is so well sited, so poised. And all around it, sitting on the low walls of the rotary on Saturdays, are young lovers smooching; not a sight one sees enough of in New York. Appropriate to this juxtaposition of Art and Life, if you continue along the Passegiata del Gianicolo, slightly below Garibaldi in elevation is the monument to his woman, Anita—a fiery Brazilian, counterpart in the independence struggle, brandishing a pistol. Not so good as sculpture, but definitely more than a footnote. It was a gift of the Brazilian people.

JUDITH SHEA
Artist

The equestrian statue of Anita is a much more dramatic monument than that of Giuseppe. She is on a rearing horse, holding a baby with one arm and a pistol with the other.

JEAN S. WEISZ
Art historian, University of California—Los Angeles

Sunday afternoon, see Italian families out with children in best clothes; *burattini* doing Punchinello scenes; children

PIAZZALE GIRABALDI

VIEW

*Seated at sunset at one of the outdoor cafes near Piazzale
Garibaldi is the only way to learn Rome with heart and soul.
There it is, its roofs spread out before you like an endless series
of terra-cotta terraces, the solid gray imminence of the Palazzo
Farnese below, the flying saucer of the Pantheon settled down
in the medieval-Renaissance city around it, the spectacular
Victor Emmanuel monument in its Brescian marble fussiness
looking like some overbred white dog with its black ears cocked,
the awesomeness of the Capitoline and Colosseum miniaturized
but unaffected, San Giovanni in Laterano a jagged crown of
saints in the distance, and beyond the blue mythology of the
Sabine and Alban Hills. The river glints in the golden light as it
pulls the Isola Tiberina, the synagogue, and the Ghetto close
into its coils while you note everything, identifying everything.
What greater delight than to spend a sunset with a map of Rome
in one hand, a Campari and soda in the other, and the city
spread out before you in all its ages and wonders?*
JANET SULLIVAN
Writer, Rhode Island School of Design

riding donkeys, ponies; stalls with souvenirs and food.
ELAINE FANTHAM
Classicist, Princeton University

For perfection, I recommend a sunset on the Janiculum
near the Garibaldi monument. Memory is served like a sul-
tan's pleasure full of dark cypress, umbrella pines, and the
colors of Corot. Layers of Trastevere's tiles, the sycamores
of the Tiber, the other hills of the smokey city join a sky of
cloudy majesty if you're lucky. Get a caffè or a gelato, sit on
the ancient wall, finish a journal entry, a sketch, a poem, a
letter, or just a thought worthy of your life.
JAMES R. TURNER
Landscape architect

8.18 **Bosco Parrasio**

via di Porta San Pancrazio 32

If you can get in you'll discover a delightful secret garden
with three levels. Originally, home to a literary society,
Arcadia, precursor to the Academia Letteraria Italiana.
CRAIG H. WALTON
Architect

8.19 **Tasso's Oak**

Monastery of Sant'Onofrio, Passegiata del
Gianicolo

A short amble past the monument to Garibaldi and on down
the Passegiata del Gianicolo leads to the celebrated literary
landmark known as Tasso's Oak. The twisted, blackened,
iron-corsetted trunk of this long-dead tree is a relic of the
Renaissance poet's last days in Rome. Tasso is said to have
planted it himself when he was living in the nearby monastery
of Sant'Onofrio. This tree, along with the monk's cell in
which he died in 1595, and his simple tomb inside the tiny
church have become shrines for many a literary pilgrimage.
Goethe, Chateaubriand, Longfellow, Henry James, and John
Cheever were just a few of those who came to what Herman
Melville called the "quaint, damp, and doleful" Sant'Onofrio
to pay their respects to the epic poet. For many authors, and
especially for romantics like Byron and Shelley, Tasso's
appeal partly lay in the kind of life he led. Melancholic,
passionate, and deeply distrustful of others, his seven-year
imprisonment at the behest of a dissatisfied patron made
him the very archetype of the alienated artist who, punished
by society for his differences, continued to create works of
enduring nobility and fame. In the monastery there is a
small Museo Tassiano with the poet's death mask, volumes
of his work, and other artifacts relating to his life.
JOHN VARRIANO
Art historian, Mount Holyoke College

8.20 **The American Academy in Rome**

via Angelo Masina 5

The American Academy, ten buildings on eleven acres of
gardens, the highest point within the walls, is interesting
and beautiful in and of itself, but especially for its associa-
tion with some of the most significant American artists and
scholars of the century.

The unusual collection of buildings and gardens includes
the fine 17th-century Villa Aurelia, which provides the formal spaces for concerts and scholarly presentations; the
Casa Rustica, a tavern-turned-studio complex for Academy
Fellows; the Bellacci, a cozy turn-of-the-century domicile
now the Director's residence; the Bass Garden, a quiet,
enclosed corner of the *campagna*; and especially, the McKim,
Mead and White–designed main building that houses the
community of Fellows and Residents. This 128-room palazzo
is colloquially known as the McKim building, although it
was designed after the Academy's famous founder had died.
Finished in 1914, it has been a nurturing place for many
great Americans, such as John Russell Pope, Samuel Barber,
Philip Guston, Nancy Graves, Robert Venturi, Michael
Graves, Lester K. Little, Frank Stella, Mary Miss, Lucy Shoe
Merritt, James Ackerman, Richard Wilbur, and many, many
others.

ADELE CHATFIELD-TAYLOR
*Historic preservationist, writer, President of the American
Academy in Rome*

ALSO RECOMMENDED BY
BERT L. LONG, JR.

8.21 **Bar Gianicolo**

  Piazzale Aurelia 5, ☎ 06 58 06 275
closed Mondays

For an early breakfast, go to the Bar-G, a stone's throw from
the Academy's front gate. Delicious coffee, a cornetto, a jolt
of pressed lemon juice; gelato in the summer.

ADELE CHATFIELD-TAYLOR

8.22 **Antico Arco**

Piazzale Aurelia 7, ☎ 06 58 15 274

An exquisite upscale restaurant with more refined fare than the traditional Roman. (Try the pappardelle with rabbit and bits of fried artichoke.)
KENNETH FRAZELLE

8.23 **Ristorante Scarpone**

via San Pancrazio 15, ☎ 06 58 14 094

To get to Scarpone at dinnertime, one must cross from the Porta San Pancrazio just when traffic is at peak, then continue along the via Aurelia, hugging the wall. If you do manage to survive, you'll find a delightful menu and careful service from waiters who have been there for years. In season, dine in the garden.
NORMA GOLDMAN

ALSO RECOMMENDED BY
SUSAN WOOD

8.24 **Villa Sciarra**

Just inside the Aurelian Wall near the stops for Bus 75 or Bus 44 in via G. Carini

An ideal small-scale gathering place on a sunny morning, where young mothers, *nonnas*, or maids take toddlers to commune with pigeons and throw gravel. Shade trees offer a choice of sitting in the sun or not. On Saturday the young fathers have the duty. Rome's teak and iron benches are in their most perfect setting. It is also a favorite hangout for *i gatti di Roma*.
A. RICHARD WILLIAMS
Visiting Professor of architecture at the University of Arizona–Tucson

From Trastevere uphill to the Janiculum

A meandering in Trastevere is filled with the delights of shopping and seeing the true Rome. Have lunch at Da Gildo—a light pizza and punterelle salad—and visit Santa Maria in Trastevere. You really can't get lost in the maze as long as you head uphill (consult a map eventually). I would plan to spend an afternoon in Trastevere and start ascending before sunset, to watch the golden light over the old city; head for the Fontana Paola. Then wander up at dinnertime to Antico Arco, an exquisite upscale restaurant with more refined fare than the traditional Roman. (Try the pappardelle with rabbit and bits of fried artichoke.) Two other neighborhood restaurants you won't find in guidebooks are also atop the Janiculum Hill: Il Cortile, with tables of delicious antipasti, and Bruno ai Quattro Venti, featuring grilled fish. If you're persuasive enough (we had to prove ourselves as regulars first) they'll bring out a dessert tray of fruttini—assorted fruit and nut gelati painstakingly stuffed in nut shells and fruit skins. *Buon appetito!*

KENNETH FRAZELLE

Composer, North Carolina School of the Arts. Composer-in-Residence for the Los Angeles Chamber Orchestra

ITINERARY

ⓐ Da Gildo, via Della Scala 31a

ⓑ Santa Maria in Trastevere

ⓒ Fontana Paola, Passeggiata del Gianicolo and via della Porta San Pancrazio

ⓓ Three restaurants on the Janiculum

- Antico Arco, Piazzale Aurelia and Porta San Pancrazio (see p. 189)

- Il Cortile, via Alberto Mario 26 (see p. 191)

- Bruno ai Quattro Venti, viale dei Quattro Venti 172a

8.25 Il Cortile

✗ via Alberto Mario 26   ☎ 06 58 03 433

Situated on the Janiculum, this is a very nice restaurant for dinner. Not cheap, but excellent food and service, and lovely atmosphere. Also open for those lingering Roman lunches.

Pamela Starr

8.26 Ristorante Antica Roma

✗ via Alberto Mario, 17, 1½ blocks east of via G. Carini
Dinner only, closed Wednesdays

A modest neighborhood place run by an Abruzzi family. Virtually no tourists.

A. Richard Williams

8.27 Villa Doria Pamphili

via di San Pancrazio

The grounds of the villa have been turned into a vast and beautiful park populated by real Romans relaxing in a setting of gardens and villa architecture. Afterwards, try
✗ dinner at the Hosteria Eden on the nearby Piazza Ottavilla.

Roger Ulrich
Classicist, Dartmouth College

There are many oases where one may seek peace from the hectic Roman scene, but few as vast as this park, incorporating the 17th-century Villa Doria Pamphili. The long views through the towering umbrella pines, planted on a grid, reintroduce nature into the incredibly urban (and relatively treeless) eternal city. On Sunday, the park's usual quietude is shattered as crowds of Romans settle in for picnic lunches and soccer games after church and passeggiate on the Gianicolo hill. The nearby park of the Villa Sciarra offers similar views on a more intimate scale.

Robert Evans
Architect

ALSO RECOMMENDED BY
MARK ADAMS, GREGORY BUCHER, ROBERT LIVESEY

Wall paintings at Columbarium of Scribonius

Menophilus, 1st century AD
Casino Algarde, in Villa Doria Pamphili

The columbarium, or underground burial chamber, was
discovered only in 1981. Because of the superior conserva-
tion methods, the frescoes look as if they were painted only
yesterday. There are theater masks, scenes from tragedy,
musical instruments, fruit, birds, and animals, including a
large brown rabbit. There is also a splendid *opus tesselatum*
(square-tiled) mosaic floor. It is only opened by special
permission, and visitors really shouldn't go down there,
since the condensation of their breath will eventually
destroy it.

FRANCESCA SANTORO L'HOIR
Classicist

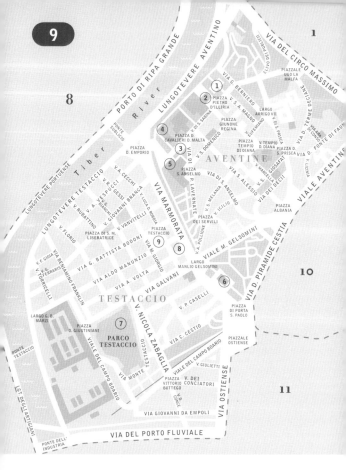

THE AVENTINE

1. Parco Savelli
2. Santa Sabina
3. Piazza dei Cavalieri di Malta
4. Santa Maria del Priorato
5. Sant'Anselmo
6. Ufficio Postale

TESTACCIO

7. Testaccio Hill
× ▮ 8. Formaggiomania
   ▮ 9. Central Market

N

THE AVENTINE

The larger setting of the hill has a monastic/early Christian
air—there's often a wedding and always scurrying monks. A
great place to stroll, great views, proximity to great pizza in
Testaccio. San Anselmo and Santa Sabina are fine examples
of early Christian medieval religious development.
CYNTHIA WHITE
Classicist, University of Arizona

9.1 **Parco Savelli**

One of the three or four best spots from which to survey the
cityscape and its ruins, rooftops, domes, and palaces, as
well as the sky above. The park itself is small and beautiful.
JENNY STRAUSS CLAY
Classicist, University of Virginia

9.2 **Santa Sabina**

5th century AD
Piazza Pietro d'Illiria 1

This early Christian basilica, one of the outstanding surviv-
iors of 5-6th century Christian art, shows its clear relations
to the ancient Roman tradition. Note, especially, the carved
wood doors.
WILLIAM E. WALLACE
Art historian, Washington University

ALSO RECOMMENDED BY
WALTER HOOD, CYNTHIA WHITE

9.3 **The Piazza dei Cavalieri di Malta**

Piranesi, 1765

The sequence of approach, the [...] of the piazza, Piranesi's
decorative details, and his seductive moves finally attract
to peeking through a keyhole. Then there's the view beyond…
PETER G. ROLLAND
Landscape Architect

RECOMMENDED READING 49, 111

9.4 Santa Maria del Priorato

Piranesi, 1764–1766
Piazza dei Cavaliere di Malta just off Piazza
Sant'Anselmo
*Admission Wednesday only, or apply to the office of the
Order of the Knights of Malta, at via Condotti 68,*
☎ *06 675 811*

The least-known masterpiece of 18th-century Rome, surviving in almost perfect condition in its seclusion amid
delectable gardens on the Aventine Hill, Santa Maria del
Priorato is the only architectural work by Piranesi. It is the
Priory church of the Knights of Malta. Visitors expecting a
work of sublime scale like Piranesi's etched monuments of
Roman antiquity will find instead a group of architectural
structures encrusted with images of arcane fantasy, inspired
by Etruscan history and the military order. The church
interior, exquisitely ornate, is dominated by the most idiosyncratic altar in Rome, watched over by Piranesi's own
funerary statue.
John Wilton-Ely
Art historian, author of Piranesi as Architect and Designer

9.5 Sant'Anselmo

Piazza Sant'Anselmo

Sung vespers

At the recommendation of someone who knows Rome well,
I went with a few friends on a Sunday evening (7:15) to Sant'
Anselmo. The church is quite new (late 19th century) but in
the Romanesque-Lombard style. Reached by a short walkway
from the piazza, it is fronted by a beautiful courtyard, gently
illuminated in the dark of a winter evening. A central fountain sparkled and babbled as we made our way into the church.
As the evening bells began to ring, the monks—about sixty-
five in all, and of all ages (arranged, it seemed, by seniority)
filed in. Each dropped his cowl upon entering the sanctuary.

For the next hour we listened to the liturgical singing of
a community that places itself within a larger and much older

community of Benedictine monks by singing the Vespers each evening at the same time. The voices were beautiful and tranquil. At the end, the monks filed back out, donning cowls at the sanctuary door. As they exited, someone began to extinguish the candles and other lights in the church, which had, as we made our way out, turned quite dark, mimicking the dimming of nature's light and the beginning of a time of rest, more prayer, and quiet. We walked, silently, out into the courtyard which had, by now, darkened. We hardly spoke. It wasn't "entertainment," but it was, as my friend had assured us, very special.

LINDA W. RUTLAND GILLISON
Classicist, University of Montana–Missoula

9.6 Ufficio Postale

Mario de Renzi and Adalberto Libera, 1933–1934
via Marmorata 4

Two masterpieces of the Fascist era are found, respectively, at the Bologna and Pyramide stops on the Metropolitana. The post office in Rome's Piazza Bologna, Mario Ridolfi's winning competition entry of 1932, faces the piazza with a sinuous façade that slides across the space with a Baroque fluidity, undulating convex against concave, like Borromini's San Carlo. Ridolfi used neutral, almost blank, penetrations and a flange canopy on the roof to emphasize the strongly horizontal curving skin of stone laid up like Roman brick.

For the same competition, Adalberto Libera and Mario De Renzi's winning design for another post office at the foot of the Aventine Hill in the via Marmorata engages in semantic play and tense formal juxtapositions that verge on the surreal. This building superimposes divergent references, as is appropriate for a project that abuts the medieval Porta San Paolo and the Pyramid of Cestius. The outer block of the building, with its white surface and the neutrality of square windows, appears to conform to a rationalist rigor. These first perceptions seem peculiarly compromised by the crossing diagonals of the spandrels and mullions in the stairwells at the block's most prominent forward extension. Held within this frame is the public hall, a glazed metal oval—a civic form

Walks on the Aventine

Start in the garden of the orange trees
(Giardino degli Aranci) for a panorama of
Rome, then on to Santa Sabina and
Sant'Alessio, with the keyhole of the
Knights of Malta (Santa Maria del
Priorato), down the hill to the English
Cemetery and the Pyramid of Caius
Cestius. Sant'Anselmo is another possible
stop. Finish with a public rose garden on
the via di Valle Murcia and a view of the
Circus Maximus.

JUNE N. STUBBS AND JOHN C. STUBBS
*Profesor of Italian and Professor of
English, Virginia Polytechnic Institute
and State University*

Walk on the Aventine Hill for a peaceful
and quiet stroll into the distant past, in the
evening with a westering sun lighting up the
Palatine Hill across the Circus Maximus.

WILLIAM E. WALLACE
Art historian, Washington University

ITINERARY

a Giardino degli
Aranci (Parco
Savelli)

b Santa Sabina,
Sant'Alessio, and
Santa Maria del
Priorato

c The English
Cemetery, Pyramid
of Caius Cestius

d Sant'Anselmo

e Public rose garden

like the nearby Circus Maximus and Piazza Navona. Its own stainless steel structure carries this object-space which protrudes glistening from within the arms of the surrounding icy stone block. In front of these elements is a portico that extends beyond the mass on either side originally in contrasting black marble. These elements do not resolve or harmonize. They collide, sitting in an adjacency typical of period photo-collage, and like that revolutionary and critical medium, they generate the friction that such adjacencies must produce.

MICHAEL STANTON
Architect

TESTACCIO

9.7 Testaccio Hill

via Galvani

One of the least of Rome's hills, Monte Testaccio is a man-made eminence that rises just a hundred feet over the surrounding streets near the Tiber south of the city. It is adjacent to what was the commercial dock area in antiquity. *Testa* is the Latin word for earthenware pottery and Monte Testaccio (*Mons Testaceus* in Latin) means "Hill of Potsherds" —an exact description of its makeup. For many years, it was built up by dumping the debris from the dock area, largely bits and pieces of broken amphoras, which became compacted over the centuries. Walking on its surface is an extraordinary experience. Plans are underway to open the hill as a park. Today the site gives its name to the gritty neighborhood and nightlife district surrounding the hill and the nearby former municipal slaughterhouse or *Mattatoio*.

PAUL PASCAL
Classicist, University of Washington

The artificial hill, an ancient landfill, was a dump for used amphoras in Roman times. By day, the hill can be climbed by entering through a gate and following an overgrown path to the top, where a fine view of Rome can be seen. If one looks closely the buried amphora shards that make up the hill can be seen along the paths. By night, a variety of live and DJ music can be heard there.

LESLIE RAINER
Conservator

9.8 Formaggiomania

✕ 🛍 via Marmorata 47, ☎ 06 57 46 986

When I go to Rome, I do the things that a visitor there usually does. That is, I look at the Caravaggios, go to the Vatican, visit the Villa Giulia. I eat out at Piperno and Vecchia Roma. I might even buy a pair of shoes. But the thing I do that most visitors probably do not is visit Formaggiomania, the best cheese store in Rome. The variety of Italian country cheeses there is unsurpassed, and one may sample as many as one likes before settling on what three or four to buy. And the breads, salame, and hams are also superb. The owner, E. Volpetti, has a little pizza place around the corner. It is perfect for a casual no-frills lunch. A terrific excursion is to walk from the Janiculum Hill down to Porta Portese and out on via Marmorata to the Protestant Cemetery, where one can check out the cats, stare a minute or two at Keats's grave, then head back to Formaggiomania for a glass or two of wine and some slices of astonishingly good pizza. After lunch, a walk over the Aventine with stops at Sant'Anselmo and Santa Sabina to Santa Maria in Cosmedin! On a clear day there is nothing better.

MARK STRAND
Poet

9.9 Central Market

🛍 Piazza di Testaccio

One of the last of a slowly vanishing 3000-year-old Roman institution. (These are disappearing because Rome's population inside the Aurelian walls is now 1/10th of what it was in Roman times—100,000 vs. 1,000,000.)

GEORGE E. HARTMAN
Architect

2

1

COLOSSEUM

PIAZZA
DEL
COLOSSEO

VIA LABICANA

VIA CELIO VIBENNA

(10)

VIA OSTILIA

V. DEI
SS. QUATTRO
MANINI

(9)

PIAZZA
S. CLEMENTE

PARCO
DEL CELIO

VIA CLAUDIA

VIA CAPO D'AFRICA

VIA M. CELIMONTANA

VIA DI S. GIOVANNI IN LATERANO

VIA DEI SS. QUATTRO CORONATI

(4)

V. CL AURELIO

VIA ANNIA

VIA DI S. GREGORIO

CLIVO (5) DI SCAURO

(6)

V. S. PAOLO D. CROCE

PIAZZA
CELIMONTANA

VIA DI S. STEFANO ROTONDO

V. DI VILLA FONSECA

PIAZZA
SAN GREGORIO

(7)

VIA DELLA NAVICELLA

(8)

VIA DI S. ERASMO

V. VALERI

VIA DELL'AMBA ARADAM

V. DRUSIANA

V. DECEN

PIAZZA
DI PORTA
CAPENA

VILLA
CELIMONTANA

VIA DI VALLE DELLE CAMENE

PIAZZA DI PORTA
METRONIA

PIAZZALE
METRONIA

V.D. FERRATELLA IN LATERANO

VIALE IPPONIO

VIA DELLE TERME DI CARACALLA

VIALE G. BACCELLI

VIALE G. BACCELLI

STADIO
DELLE
TERME

VIA ANTONINA

VIA DRUSO

VIALE METRONIO

PARCO
DI PORTA
CAPENA

PIAZZA
DI S. BALBINA

V. DI S. BALBINA

PIAZZALE NUMA
POMPILIO

V. E. ROSA

SAN GIOVANNI IN LATERANO AND VICINITY

1. Santa Croce in Gerusalemme
2. San Giovanni in Laterano
3. Basilica di Porta Maggiore

THE CELIAN HILL

4. Santi Quattro Coronati
5. Celian Hill and Clivus Scauri

6. Arcades of the Temple of Deified Claudius
7. San Gregorio Magno
8. Santo Stefano Rotondo
9. San Clemente
× 10. Ristorante Pasqualino

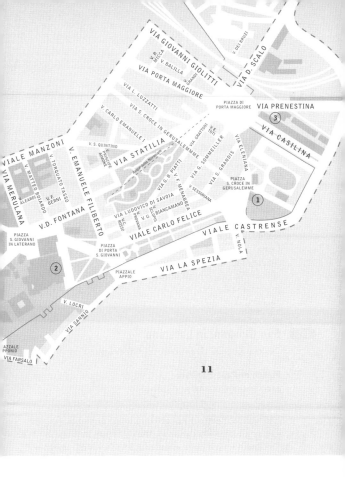

11

SAN GIOVANNI IN LATERANO AND VICINITY

10.1 Santa Croce in Gerusalemme
viale Carlo Felice

Take the Number 13 tram out to the church of Santa Croce, which holds the treasures that Saint Helena, mother of Constantine the Great, brought back from the Holy Land. See up close a thorn from Christ's crown of thorns. See wood from the true cross. See the actual nails that crucified Christ. Best of all, see the actual finger of Saint Thomas—yes, the very finger that the doubting saint poked into the side of the living Jesus after the Resurrection.
JOHN GUARE
Playwright

10.2 San Giovanni in Laterano
Piazza di San Giovanni in Laterano

Fresco of Pope Boniface
attributed to Giotto, c. 1300

Reopenings and completed restorations are among the many gifts the Jubilee Year has given to Rome and to its visitors—just as jubilees have done for the city since its first, in 1300. The small fresco fragment shows Boniface VIII, the pope Dante loved to hate, declaring the first Jubilee in 1300—an appropriate patron, perhaps, of travelers to Rome in the "Giubileo 2000." It is on the inner aisle, on the south side of the church.
LINDA W. RUTLAND GILLISON
Classicist, University of Montana

Baptistery of San Giovanni in Fonte
Constantine, 4th century AD; Sixtus III, 5th century
Piazza di San Giovanni in Laterano
open daily; ask sacristan to unlock the chapels

Unique assemblage of late-antique architecture and splendid mosaics in the chapels of Santi Rufina and Seconda, San

Venanzio, and Saint John the Evangelist. One would, naturally, combine this visit with the Basilica of San Giovanni in
Laterano, its lovely cloister, and the Scala Santa. Also cast a
glance at the obelisk of Tutmose III from Thebes, shipped to
Rome by Constantius II (357 AD). Remember that the equestrian statue of Marcus Aurelius, now at the Campidoglio,
once stood here.

Elfriede and Georg Knauer
Consulting scholar, University Museums, University of
Pennsylvania; Classicist, University of Pennsylvania

RECOMMENDED READING 64

Sancta Sanctorum (Chapel of St. Lawrence)
Pope Nicholas III, 1278
Piazza di San Giovanni in Laterano

This private chapel is a perfect jewel box filled with important religious relics and marble work. The site is all that
remains of the old papal palace destroyed by Sixtus V as part
of his urban renewal project in the 16th century.
June N. Stubbs and John C. Stubbs
Professor of Italian; Professor of English, Virginia
Polytechnic Institute and State University

10.3 Basilica di Porta Maggiore
via Prenestina, just outside the Porta Maggiore
for admission, call the Soprintendenza di Beni Culturali
e Ambientali, ☎ 06 67 03 03

This often-ignored or perhaps forgotten 1st-century basilica
is extraordinary in the proportions of the nave and the decoration of its surfaces. An underground structure once used
by a secret society, it was discovered in 1917 upon the building of Rome's modern railroad. It is a wonderful example
not only of basilican architecture but also of exquisite low-
relief stucco work. The entire interior surface, now extant
primarily in the ceiling, was gridded into squares in which
various mythic stories are depicted. The mythic figures
appear purposefully "too small" within their frames and
thereby convey an almost primitive but wonderful sense of

The Seven Pilgrimage Churches

Spend an entire Sunday from dawn to dusk, like good pilgrims, visiting all seven of the papal basilicas.

MARY ANN MELCHERT
American Academy in Rome. 1984–1988

ITINERARY

a San Sebastiano, via Appia Antica 136

b San Giovanni in Laterano, Piazza San Giovanni in Laterano, via Merulana

c Santa Croce in Gerusalemme, Piazza Santa Croce, viale Carlo Felice

d San Lorenzo fuori le Mura, Piazzale del Verano 3, via Tiburtina

e Santa Maria Maggiore, Piazza di Santa Maria Maggiore, via Merulana

f San Pietro, Piazza San Pietro

g San Paolo fuori le Mura, via Ostiense 186 (San Paolo stop on Metro line "B")

The experienced visitor to Rome, who might well feel as if return is a pilgrimage, should at least once make a circuit of the seven Pilgrimage Churches: San Sebastiano, San Giovanni in Laterano, Santa Croce in Gerusalemme, San Lorenzo fuori le Mura, Santa Maria Maggiore, San Pietro, and San Paolo fuori le Mura. These will give you the full range of Roman styles, from early Christian catacombs to 19th-century updating and post–World War II reconstructions, and everything in between. The middle five can be done in one very long walk, and if you are heroic enough to add the others at the beginning and the end, you deserve the best dinner that Passetto (via Zanardelli 14, ☎ 06 68 80 6569) can provide you.

VIRGINIA L. BUSH
Art historian

perspective. This distortion of size also occurs in Roman wall painting, but here there is a double reading—of figures seen in the distance and of a medallion like decoration of the gridded framework.

MICHAEL GRAVES
Architect

Campo Verano

next to the Basilica of San Lorenzo fuori le Mura in the Piazzale del Verano (not shown on map)

Begun in the mid-19th century, the main cemetery of Rome gives a history of modern Italy through its monuments and memorials for the dead. Incorporating life-size Victorian sculptures of virginal youth, memorials to the deceased of two world wars, and small enameled photographs of loved ones lighted by eternal (incandescent) flames, the "Field of Summer" gives a flavor of the social history of Romans and how they see themselves. Take a picnic lunch.

ROBERT EVANS
Architect

Aurelian Wall

Museo delle Mura
via di Porta San Sebastiano 18
(not shown on map), ☎ 06 70 47 52 84

Rome's imposing city walls, most of which date from the later 3rd century AD, can be visited in many spots and emerge constantly and unexpectedly from the cityscape in different neighborhoods. They were begun by the emperor Aurelian in the year 271, and built very quickly, when the declining empire was subject to increasing threat of attack by Goth and Vandal barbarians. Twelve miles long and about twenty to thirty feet high with evenly spaced towers and elaborate marble gates, the Aurelian Wall was maintained up through the Renaissance.

One way to experience the wall close up is to visit the small Museo delle Mura at Porta San Sebastiano. The museum itself is rather bare; it includes scale models and photographs of the walls. But its most interesting feature is the opportunity it gives to prowl through the rooms built into the ancient forti-fied gate, as well as a promenade along a section of the wall.

Here one can share, somewhat eerily, the point of view of the defenders. Nine towers are included in the walk; they are connected by narrow passageways, with many steep steps. Pieces of more ancient marble with Latin inscriptions can be seen incorporated into the 3rd-century brickwork, and there are glimpses of the street below through the narrow slits provided for archers.

PAUL PASCAL
Classicist, University of Washington

THE CELIAN HILL

10.4 Santi Quattro Coronati

via dei Santi Quattro Coronati

This fortified church, a defense bastion for the Lateran basilica and palace, is a splendid example of the many layers of time to be found in a single site in Rome. The free-standing Chapel of San Silvestro contains 13th-century frescoes (well restored) of the legend of Constantine. The church proper is a good place to see a Baroque interior in a medieval building, with some very typical Roman painting, medieval floor, inscrip-tions, etc. The cloister (my favorite in Italy) is astounding for its peace, architecture, and mélange of ancient and medieval objects and contains Carolingian architectural elements.

CHARLES WITKE
Classicist, University of Michigan

ALSO RECOMMENDED BY
ELFRIEDE AND GEORG KNAUER, LYDIA LENAGHAN

10.5 Celian Hill and Clivus Scauri

off via San Gregorio to Piazza di Santi Giovanni e Paolo

This whole treasury on the Celian Hill, from Santo Stefano

Rotondo with its lurid murals; the walks near the 16th-century Villa Celimontana; the Cosmati mosaics on the Navicella (at Santa Maria in Dominica); the restored Roman rooms under Santi Giovanni and Paolo; the piazza; and the lowest monastery of San Gregorio Magno, give the purest glimpse into the past. The cypresses, the open spaces filled with gardens, birds, bridal parties—but no cars—are rare.

ROBERT HAMILTON
Painter

10.6 Arcades of the Temple of Deified Claudius

begun 54 AD
Piazza dei Santi Giovanni e Paolo
Ring at the convent next to Santi Giovanni e Paolo for permission to enter.

Built to support the Temple of Claudius, this portico is remarkable both for its enormous scale and as a precursor for Mannerism. These arcades have giant order columns, large keystones, and pronounced rustication. The similarity to work a millenium and a half later is eerie. One can only imagine Giulio Romano, Michelangelo, and others standing in amazement before this piece of archaeology—looking into their own future.

ROBERT KAHN
Architect

10.7 San Gregorio Magno

575 AD, *rebuilt by Giovanni Battista Soria, 1629–1633*
Piazza di San Gregorio

I'd recommend this for the unusual flatness of the church; don't miss the three chapels in the adjoining garden.

ROBERT LIVESEY
Architect, Director, Knowlton School of Architecture, Ohio State University

10.8 **Santo Stefano Rotondo**

late 5th century
via di Santo Stefano 7

If you find yourself in need of rest and solitude—if Rome's
brilliant colors, grand spaces, and splendid forms have
exhausted your eyes—consider spending a few hours at Santo
Stefano Rotondo. It is a secluded church on the Celian Hill,
hardly ever visited by tourists. The incessant, frenetic pace
of Rome comes to a beautiful standstill inside its white-
washed walls.

Santo Stefano Rotondo has no great vistas or progressions,
no dramatic perspectival views to suggest dynamic movement.
The shape of its interior—a simple circle—conveys a sense
of deep peace and serenity. Like Rome's martyria—Santa
Costanza, the Tempietto at San Pietro in Montorio—Santo
Stefano circles around a bit of ground and transforms it into a
sacred center. The meaning of this center is symbolic: unlike
true martyria, the church does not mark the physical site of
Saint Stephen's execution. This first martyr of the Faith was
stoned to death far from here, outside the walls of Jerusalem.

In its original form, as built by Pope Simplicius, Santo
Stefano's circular plan was overlaid by a Greek cross: four
equal chapels projected crosswise beyond the present ambulatory. Nicholas V and his architect Leon Battista Alberti
purged Santo Stefano of its side chapels. The interior became
even simpler, closer in its roundness to the mythical "Center
of the Ideal City" envisioned by Renaissance artists such as
Piero della Francesca. It also came to resemble ancient Rome's
circular tombs (Augustus, Hadrian, Cecilia Metella). Yet
while their chambers are tight and confining, there is soar-
ing breadth and emptiness inside Santo Stefano: the center
space, defined by slender Ionic columns, is a full twenty-two
meters wide and equally tall. The clerestory walls of this
majestic drum are pure, white plaster, their only decoration
a row of eleven round-arched windows. A wide ambulatory
with a simple wood floor envelops the central space—its
generous breadth and slow curvature make this one of Rome's
gentlest, most leisurely interior walkways.

Like most Roman buildings, Santo Stefano does have its

Christmas Eve Masses

With a bit of planning, and a little luck, it is possible to attend portions of three notable midnight Masses on a single Christmas Eve—one at St. Peter's, another at the Church of San Giovanni in Laterano (the Lateran), and yet another at San Clemente. You'll need a car or motorino, a map of Rome, and familiarity with the route (this can be achieved by rehearsing the drive between Vatican City and the Lateran, and the Lateran and San Clemente).

It's necessary to buy tickets in advance for the midnight Mass at Saint Peter's. Park your car on the east side of Vatican City to avoid driving all the way around it on your way to the Lateran. After you arrive at St. Peter's, try to stand in the back on the right behind the barrier that creates the aisle across the rear of the basilica. There you will be within a few feet of the procession and the Pope as they begin their march toward the altar. (There is speculation that sometimes the Vatican uses a stand-in for the real Pope. You might be able to confirm this for yourself by seeing the Pope perform the Stations of the Cross at the Colosseum at Easter.) This spot also provides for an easy exit, which you should make after you have seen enough (in any case, no later than shortly after the end of the procession has reached the altar and the Pope seems to be only about one inch tall). With a little luck you will arrive at the Lateran in time to see the procession of the living Crêche from the baptistery to the church. If you are too late, don't miss the Crêche tableau, which follows the Mass, with its live baby Jesus, little-girl angels, and a light show that might remind you of a late 1960s high school dance.

On to San Clemente to catch the music at the end of that Mass—and perhaps a new appreciation for the elegance and modesty of medieval church architecture. ➤

If you manage to successfully negotiate the entire agenda you will have spent an evening contemplating incredible architectural and spiritual contrasts. You will also have the sense of accomplishment of having orchestrated a complicated itinerary that requires luck and a gut sense of timing. You might be left wondering on Christmas morning if fate, chance, or some other force had intervened to make your venture a success.

Don't forget, six days later on New Year's Eve, to eat a hearty portion of lentils to ensure your financial future and complete your Roman holiday.

Matthew Geller
Artist

Buy tickets in advance for midnight Mass at St. Peter's by calling the Prefettura della Casa Ponteficia, ☎ *06 69 88 30 17; 06 69 88 3114*

oddities—strange features that contrast sharply with its original design. One of them is the three-columned structure
carrying arches that spans the central drum, dividing it into
two halves. Its purpose may have been to distinguish between
an altar area and a congregation space. It is a wonder that
this audacious gesture—a line slicing through the very center
of the interior—does not in fact detract from the circular
plan. A much more discordant feature is the cycle of Counter-
Reformation frescoes by Nicolo Circignani (known as Il
Pomarancio). They show gruesome scenes of torture and
death, their savageness quite at odds with the soothing, still
interior of Santo Stefano. The frescoes moved Charles
Dickens to write, "Such a panorama of horror and butchery
no man could imagine in his sleep, though he were to eat a
whole pig, raw, for supper." Here is perhaps the greatest
mismatch between artwork and architecture in Rome. Thank-
fully, the frescoes are pale in color and can, if one wishes it,
be ignored. Santo Stefano remains, despite these bloody
paintings, a miraculously serene and peaceful interior.
SANDA D. ILIESCU
Artist, designer

There are two early Christian buildings I regard as twin "must-
see" sites because their innovative spaces reflect the dynamic
shape of the urban landscape of Rome. Both the Church of
Santo Stefano Rotondo and that of Santa Costanza (see p.
49) have circular plans that evoke the round temples of pagan
Rome and the monumental ellipses of Imperial amphithe-
aters, stadia, and circuses. These Imperial sites of spectacle
inscribe the circle in the future plan of Rome, e.g., the Piazza
Navona descends from Domitian's Stadium. Any visitor's
walk through Rome is marked by surprise encounters with
grand ovoid spaces and by the theatrical convex and concave
façades of the Baroque. When we walk into the bounded circles of the churches their silent darkened spaces offer a
meditation on the dynamic public passages just left outside.
CHRISTINE KONDOLEON
Curator of Greek and Roman Art, Worcester Art Museum

ALSO RECOMMENDED BY
JOSEPH CONNORS, LYNN KEARNEY

10.9 **San Clemente**

via di San Giovanni in Laterano

This place, like no other, impresses upon the visitor how Rome was built over and over again on top of itself, and used bits and pieces of its former self, too—in the pavement of the upper church, for instance, ancient funerary stones are used indiscrimately as floor tiles. It also happens to sell the best postcards (derived from the mosaics) in town.
Katharine Brophy Dubois
Historian

I love the sound of the rushing water you hear as you descend, letting you know there are other layers below.
David Mayernik
Architect and fresco painter

Some 300 yards from the Colosseum stands this sublime, ancient church dedicated to Saint Clement, the third successor of Saint Peter. It is a veritable architectural palimpsest of Roman history. Descending to the third and lowest level, some thirty feet beneath the present church, one has glimpses of both pagan Rome and the very beginnings of the Christian city. By 385, a Christian church—remnants of which survive—existed on this site, but next to it, in a brick apartment house, was a Mithraic temple dating from the late 2nd century AD. Its altar, depicting Mithras sacrificing a bull to Apollo, is still there. In the 4th century the ground floors of both the apartment house and the church were filled in and architects built a new, grander Christian sanctuary atop them. In this chamber there is the palpable presence of the last days of ancient, Imperial Rome and the new triumphant power of the Christian Church. A regal fresco, for example, of the wife of the emperor Justinian, Theodora, who died in 548, has been, by the addition of the Christ Child, transformed into an image of the Madonna. Throughout this sanctuary the frescoes—including one showing the transfer of Saint Clement's body from St. Peter's to this church—are of an extraordinary quality. In 1084, during the sack of Rome by the Normans, the 4th-century church was badly damaged, and in 1108 it was decided to build a new church.

The old church, just as the first church had been, was filled
in and a new edifice erected atop it. It is this structure, typically basilican in form, with a nave, a large apse, and aisles
separated from the nave by two rows of seven columns,
which the visitor now enters through a small 12th-century
courtyard off the Piazza di San Clemente. The interior decoration of San Clemente embraces almost every period of
Christian art, from the majestic mosaic of the Crucifixion
behind the high altar, which expresses a 4th-century con-
ception of the Cross as the Tree of Life, to the Chapel of St.
Catherine with its frescos of the life of the saint painted in
the first quarter of the 15th century by Masolino da Panicale
with help from his pupil Masaccio, to the Tomb of Cardinal
Veniero (died 1479), from the School of Mino da Fiesole. To
enter San Clemente is to be enveloped with nearly 2000 years
of Roman history.

David Garrard Lowe
Art historian, author

One of the great apse mosaics of Rome, reflecting the revival
of mosaic art in Italy by Abbot Desiderius of Monte Cassino
at the end of the 11th century; the central plan marble choir
enclosure of the 12th century incorporating 6th-century
carving elements. Chapel of St. Catherine with incredible
frescoes of Masolino from about 1430; note the lower church
of the 5th century, with medieval fresco remains and the
tomb of Saint Cyril, inventor of the Cyrillic alphabet for
writing Russian.

Charles Witke
Classicist, University of Michigan

San Clemente pastes up a *bricolage* of eras. While other
buildings vie strongly with it in this regard, none quite
yields up a composite as manifold yet organic-seeming as
does this pile.

John Peck
Jungian analyst, poet

At the lowest level are the fascinating Mithraic rooms, with
the altar and triclinium, the *schola*, and always the sound of
rushing waters on their way to the Cloaca Maxima in the Tiber

bank. This is the best introduction I know to the archaeo-
logical "rabbit-hole" of Rome.
Helen F. North
Classicist, Swarthmore College

Note the stupendous apse mosaic showing the cross flower-
ing into the Tree of Life.
Ursula Heibges
Classicist, Middlebury College

This is the building that best represents for me the architectural palimpsest that is Rome. Nowhere is the historical
stratification more amazing and varied.

Already from the exterior one can see the incongruous
juxtaposition of the 12th-century Romanesque massing of
the overall structure with a late Baroque restructuring by
Carlo Fontana (1713–1719). The small brick and stone porch
is composed of elements from the 8th or 9th century with
antique Roman capitals. This leads to the rare Quadriporticum,
the only one existing in Rome, also composed of classical
columns with Ionic capitals.

Aside from the obvious 18th-century alterations in the
interior (richly carved ceilings, stucco work, and frescoes),
the nave conserves its early 12th-century character with a
fabulously elaborate Cosmatesque mosaic floor. The Schola
Cantorum, or Byzantine central choir, which had been saved
from the 4th-century basilica on this same site, is almost
completely intact. It had originally been commissioned by
Pope John II (533–535), and his monogram can still be seen
on various carved elements. The mismatched columns of
the nave, some of which are fluted and some not, have all
been taken from other classical buildings.

The elegant 12th-century ciborium supported by columns
in the presbytery is often attributed to Arnolfo di Cambio.
In the apse is the great "Triumph of the Cross" mosaic,
also from the first half of the 12th century, with a central
Crucifixion and twelve doves symbolizing the Apostles while
deer drink from springs emanating from the bottom of the
cross. In the lower fascia, Christ, the Agnus Dei, is surrounded by twelve sheep—again representing the Apostles.

Just to the right of the presbytery is the wonderful Gothic
wall tabernacle, dated 1299, which shows Boniface VIII presenting his nephew to the Virgin. This has also been attributed
to Arnolfo.

As if this were not enough, at the opposite end of the
church, to the right of the entrance, is the Chapel of Saint
Catherine, which contains a fresco cycle by Masolino with
the possible collaboration of Masaccio. At this point, any
visitor is usually reeling from the discovery of so many treasures and will probably stumble into the sacristy to buy a few
postcards. That's when you see the stairway leading down to
the remarkable excavations below the basilica. On the way
down, there are a few Roman sarcophagi embedded in the
wall. It is curious to note that the relief carving is all well
finished except for the heads in the center. This apparently
indicates that the tombs were unsold. That is, a prospective
buyer would view the more-or-less finished items and only
upon purchase would the portrait be executed.

In the narthex of the lower basilica, which many scholars
date to the 4th century, are two much-deteriorated frescoes
of the 9th and 11th centuries and, inside the nave, to the left
of the entrance, are barely legible Byzantine frescoes representing Leo IV with the square halo of the living—meaning
they were made during his papacy between 847 and 855. The
spaces between the columns in the nave have been walled
up to support the church above and midway down this wall
are two frescoes, one of which, from the early 11th century,
is called *The Legend of Sisinnio*. It represents an obscure
miracle by Saint Clement in which, in order to escape capture, he causes his pursuers to mistake some columns lying
on the ground for himself. The fresco records the dialogue
between the men trying to lift the columns (that they think
are Clement) and the written words constitute the earliest
known example of Italian as distinct from Latin. It seems
only fitting that this first recorded phrase contains a common curse and that it is recorded inside a church. *"Fili dele
pute, traite, Gosmari, Albertel, traite. Falite dereto colo palo,
Carvoncelle,"* or roughly, "Come on, you sons of bitches, pull;
come on, Gosmari, Albertello, pull. Carvoncello, you put
that lever under it."

By tram to Porta Maggiore

Take the tram from viale Trastevere to Porta Maggiore.
The trams themselves are at least thirty or forty years old,
and much smaller and creakier than other Roman buses,
with wooden seats. The number 13B travels over the Ponte
Sublicio and down via Marmorata past the Fascist-era
post office and then the Pyramid of Cestius. It then travels
down the shady viale Aventino, past the Circo Massimo, and
behind the ruins on the Palatine Hill toward the Colosseum,
on via di San Gregorio. After passing the Colosseum, you
turn up via Labicana and a little later pass by San Giovanni
in Laterano and then down via Carlo Felice past the surprising rococo façade of Santa Croce in Gerusalemme.
A few blocks later you are at Porta Maggiore.

Porta Maggiore today includes a stunning marble gate
built by Claudius in 52 AD within large sections of the
Claudian aqueduct. The piazza is webbed over with suspended tram cables and there is a fair amount of traffic
but the effect isn't diminished. Roman paving stones pass
under the arches, and just outside the gate is the curious
marble Baker's Tomb, with round ovenlike openings and
carvings of breadmaking scenes.

If you don't descend there and turn back, the tram line
continues through the San Lorenzo neighborhood where
crumbling Roman walls adjoin more modern buildings
damaged by Allied bombing in 1943. Another good spot
to get off is at the basilica of San Lorenzo fuori le Mura
(itself rebuilt after being bombed) and the entrance to the
cemetery of Campo Verano. San Lorenzo is an extraordinary 13th-century basilica built by knocking down the
apses of two smaller churches from the 4th and 5th centuries and combining them into one.

PABLO CONRAD
Writer and editor

At the end of the nave on the left, a stairway descends yet another level to a series of Roman structures from the first century. During construction, the vaults of these rooms were supported with wooden boards until the masonry and cement dried. The wood grain of these boards can still be read imprinted in the cement. The other remarkable aspect of this area is the presence of an intact Mithraeum, a 3rd-century underground room dedicated to the cult of Mithra, the Iranian sun god. This cult was suppressed around the end of the 4th century, after the legalization of Christianity under Constantine. There are curious similarities between the two cults: Mithra was supposedly born December 25; both cults had ritual ceremonies involving bread and wine, blood and water. The Mithraic altar still stands in this room; on one side a relief carving shows the god slaying a bull. While exploring these spaces, one becomes aware of the presence of water and the sound of water flowing. This underground river flows continuously and may come from a hidden spring. It has also been suggested that it comes from an aqueduct built to supply these 1st-century buildings. You are standing thirty feet below street level.

George Bisacca
Conservator of paintings, Metropolitan Museum of Art

ALSO RECOMMENDED BY
Rudolf Arnheim, Lidia Matticchio Bastianich, Robert P. Bergman, Andrea Callard, Robert Campbell, Joseph Connors, Simon Dinnerstein, Elaine Fantham, Alan Feltus, Richard Frank, Barbara Goldsmith, David M. Halperin, Gary R. Hilderbrand, Martie Holmer, Lynn Kearney, Kenneth D. S. Lapatin, James M. Lattis, David Marsh, Ann McCoy, Susan Molesky, Franc Palaia, Gerda S. Panofsky, Ernst Pulgram, Theodore K. Rabb, Pamela Starr, John H. Thow, Charles Wuorinen

RECOMMENDED READING 21, 22, 41, 51, 60, 106

10.10 Ristorante Pasqualino

via dei Santi Quattro Coronati 66, ☎ 06 70 04 576

The food is excellent, the service is friendly, and the atmosphere is unpretentious. It's right near the heart of the city, on one of the streets leading from the Colosseum, so near where tourists are likely to find themselves at lunchtime. But although it's just a short walk from the Colosseum, the Forum, and the Palatine, the location is very quiet and pleasant, away from the tourist hubbub.

SUSAN WOOD

OUTSIDE THE CITY

11

OUTSIDE OF ROME

Via Appia

This now abandoned roadway is surrounded by detritus from several millennia, including the present age. Building and sculptural fragments exist in a much lower density than in Rome, allowing them to be viewed as distant objects in the beautiful setting.
Walter Chatham
Architect

Walk it from end to end (three miles). Classical landscape, cypresses, catacombs. Bring lunch, sit in a field, and dream of the 18th-century travelers that made this part of their tour.
Ross Anderson
Architect

Pack wine and snacks, drive out the via Appia at sunset; pure Rome, no tourists; the most romantic spot outside the city. For this, as for the city in general, rent a motorino. Forget the price; there is no better way to cover the city, especially if time is a factor. Drive around both during the early morning and at twilight. It is a bit dangerous but exhilarating, unforgettable, and very Roman. I always rent a motorino, even if I am in Rome for only a day. Rent a helmet, too.
Steven Brooke
Architectural photographer and writer

RECOMMENDED READING 108

Frescoes of the Via Latina Catacomb

4th century
via Latina
By appointment only through the Vatican Commission of the Catacombs, ☎ *06 44 65 610*

For a catacomb visit, those of San Callisto or San Sebastiano, on the Appian Way, are the best. San Callisto features a 3rd-century AD funerary chapel (*cubicolo*) for the burial of the early popes and 5th-century frescoes in the so-called Santa Cecilia chapel (legend has it that Saint Cecilia was buried here).

San Sebastiano shows the long utilization of the same spot through the centuries: two 2nd-century Roman villas with frescoes, a quarry later reused as a cemetery for pagan and then Christian burials in the 3rd century, a Christian catacomb, and, in the 4th century, a funerary basilica with hundreds of tombs dug into the floor.

The "Ipogeo" or via Latina Catacomb is one of the most spectacular catacombs in Rome. Unfortunately, it is very difficult to see, being privately owned and only open by appointment. The catacomb is completely covered with perfectly preserved frescoes of exceptional quality representing scenes from the Old and New Testaments, as well as pagan subjects such as Hercules, Alcestis, etc.

ARTHUR LEVERING
Composer

Often called the "Sistine Chapel of the Early Christian world" the frescoes of the Via Latina Catacomb display a wealth of subjects painted in an often robust classic style. A relatively small ensemble with Christian and pagan *cubicla* side by side. A truly astounding site.

ROBERT P. BERGMAN (1945–1999)
Director, Cleveland Museum of Art (1993–1999)

ALSO RECOMMENDED BY
PAMELA STARR

Catacombs of Priscilla and Saint Agnes

via Salaria

The frescoes in the Priscilla Catacombs are fresh, representative, and not so well known or visited as those on the Appian Way.

CYNTHIA WHITE
Classicist, University of Arizona

Tomb of Pomponius Hylas

20 AD
via di Porta Latina 10

The columbarium was a family or group tomb named for its dovecote shape: a circular chamber with niches for urns in the walls and in the central column supporting the roof. This one is the most immaculately preserved, with painted stucco and glass mosaic decoration. It is just inside the city limits, on the way out to the Via Appia Antica from the Circus Maximus. An attendant from the nearby Tomb of the Scipios will let you inside for a 3000 lire tip, or apply for permission by calling the Comune di Roma, Ripartizione X, ☎ 06 67 10 20 70.

WENDY MOONAN
Journalist

The Three Columbaria of the Vigna Codini

1st century BC to 1st century AD
on private property near the Columbarium of Pomponius Hylas
open only with permission

These colossal semi-underground chambers are simply amazing. The columbarium discovered in 1840, for instance, has space for 700 cinerary urns. Its inscriptions are still in place (with the exception of three which have been stolen). They provide eloquent testimony of the commemorative customs of the "nobodies" of the Roman Empire—the ordinary people who didn't make it into the historical accounts of Tacitus.

FRANCESCA SANTORO L'HOIR
Classicist

✕ Cecilia Metella

via Appia Antica 125, ☎ 06 513 67 43, 511 02 13

Hillside location in large garden, ivy pergola with a splendid view of the tomb of Cecilia Metella. Setting is surprisingly countrylike, considering the closeness of the

city. Very good food, not fancy. A place where Roman families celebrate festive occasions.
Elfriede and Georg Knauer

✕ Hostaria Antica Roma

via Appia Antica, ☎ 06 51 32 888

This restaurant is the perfect place for lunch while visiting the sites of via Appia Antica. It is warm in winter and has a shaded garden in summer. The food is good, the house wine is quite good, but the atmosphere is truly entertaining. Dean Martin sings, the waiters tell jokes you can almost understand, and if you are lucky enough to be there for a holiday there will be crepe paper and balloons. Our favorite song played—"Standing on the corner watching all the girls go by."
Pamela Keech

The Ardeatine Caves

via Ardeatina 174, ☎ 06 513 67 42

A moving site commemorating the execution of innocent Romans by the Nazis in 1944. The memorial consists of graves (sarcophagi) of several hundred victims, sculpture by Mirko Basaldella and Francesco Coccia.
Al Blaustein
Painter, printmaker, Professor of Fine Arts at Pratt Institute

ALSO RECOMMENDED BY
Maria Philips

RECOMMENDED READING 94

The Nymphaeum of Egeria

2nd century AD
via Appia Pignatelli

Location: About 20 minutes by car from Rome, on the via Appia Pignatelli, which branches off the Appian Way. The visit requires wandering through tall grass and poppies and listening for the sound of running water, which is the nymphaeum.

Directions: Go through the Porta San Sebastiano and follow the Appian Way (via Appia Antica) until the second kilometer. The road bifurcates. Follow the left fork which is the via Appia Pignatelli. Following via Pignatelli keep your eyes peeled to the left and at some point you will see a small signpost which says San Urbano. It is a very sharp left. You will probably miss the turn or the sign the first try. Turn left and follow the dirt road to the end (four minutes or less). At the end is a large gate to a villa. Park your car, and walk to the right of the gate and enclosing fence. Follow the path down and around to the back of the villa which is now above as you are walking down a slope. Soon the path bears around to the left. Bear left and listen for the faint sound of water. At some point you will hear running water and emerge into the semiruined nymphaeum of Egeria.

Description: "Nymphaeum" is another word for fountain. (The nymphaeum is the inspiration and source for the bottled spring water Egeria, whose label includes a picture of the ruined nymphaeum.) Nymphaea functioned as cooling retreats from the hot summer sun. Architecturally this room is of a rectilinear plan. The room was barrel-vaulted (now semicollapsed), carved into the hillside, and a giant niche was and is the focus of this space. The spring water still issues forth from this niche and flows around a reclining male statue (probably the lid from a sarcophagus). The water spills and courses into a now ruined trough which surrounded the central space of the fountain room. The effect must have been as if one were standing or reclining on a detached piece of ground, or as if one were on an island. The two long walls flanking the niche wall each have vestiges of smaller niches which must have displayed sculpture and running water. There was no wall opposite the giant niche wall as the room opened up onto the countryside. The varying sounds that still and rushing water produce would surely have made this fountain room a very alluring and cooling precinct. Moss and vegetation would have further enhanced this chamber's cooling effects.

Background: The nymphaeum was built in the 2nd century
AD, for or by Herodes Atticus, a man of letters and patronage
from the time of Marcus Aurelius. He built his villa and park
on a a piece of property belonging to the family of his wife,
Annia Regilla. This land seems to have been designated as
the "Pagus Triopio" or the "Triopion." It has been speculated
that the park and its architectural follies were constructed
by Herodes as tokens of his love for his wife. These architectural pieces not only included the nymphaeum, but also a
small rounded tempietto (lost, but engraved by Pirro Ligorio
in the 16th century)and an exotic pavilion (also lost) whose
roof was supported by caryatids and had a flavor of chinois-
erie (engraved in the 18th century by Piranesi). And finally,
also engraved by Piranesi was the Temple of Ceres, Faustina,
and Regilla, now the medieval church of San Urbano. (Ring
the bell to the left of the villa gate and ask for permission to
visit.)

Why go here: First one has to have a passion for nymphaea
and ruins. Secondly, one has to accept dustiness, tall grass,
and a moment of anxiety that will occur when you begin to
think you are lost. What a relief when you finally hear the
water. Thirdly, like many ruins there is not a whole lot there,
but if the pleasure of ruins is your second nature you will be
in heaven.

Judith DiMaio
Architect, Yale University

RECOMMENDED READING 18, 70

Park of Aqueduct Ruins / Parco degli Aquedotti

southeast of Rome, take Metro line "A" subway to
the Giulio Agricola stop

This "park" is the intersection of the two major aqueducts
to Rome: Aqua Claudia and Aqua Marcia (Tepula and Julia
added). Also intersecting is the ancient via Latina, two rail-
roads, and two modern roads. The park has had squatter
gardens for centuries and those are still there, maintained
by people living in the nightmarish maze of low-income

housing projects that stretch for blocks before the park. Numerous ruins of villas, tombs, roads, etc. are covered in weeds and vines, coexisting with sheep, picnickers, and joggers. This is a fantastic place to get a temporal perspective on Rome and being human.

Paul DiPasquale
Sculptor

The landscape is ideal in spring and early summer. One sees ancient Rome and modern Rome crisscrossing each other in an incredible juxtaposition. Aqua Claudia, Aqua Felice, and sections of a third aqueduct are visible. A unique setting in all the world. Spend a day, have a picnic, jog, play tennis, or ride a bicycle; take lots of pictures.

Franc Palaia
Painter, photographer, muralist, curator

RECOMMENDED READING 2, 3

TIVOLI

Hadrian's Villa / Villa Adriana

Hadrian, 2nd century AD
via Tiburtina, 23 miles east of Rome
☎ 0774 53 02 03

One of the most consistently influential complexes in history since its rediscovery.

George E. Hartman
Architect

The epitome of perfection in both building and urban design can still be enjoyed in a day trip to explore Hadrian's Villa, the largest and richest Imperial villa in the Roman Empire and his chosen residence. The emperor's works here and elsewhere in Rome were inspired by Egyptian and Greek traditions. He built and rebuilt as a continuator and early preservationist. His architectural concepts and vision have perpetuated the use of constructed garden areas, the inter-

play of water with art and architecture, and the use of porticos, peristyles, and arcades.
Emily M. Whiteside
Consultant on the arts, preservation, and design

Hadrian's Villa is quiet, with a romantic atmosphere; a unique monument and historically important. One cannot imagine the size of the palace without walking through it. Virtual reality will not do here. It gives the scale in which Roman autocrats lived and thought.
Charles K. Williams II
Archaeologist, emeritus director of the Corinth excavation, American School of Classical Studies, Athens

Gives an indelible impression of the life and imagination of the emperor and also of the most creative aspects of Roman architecture.
James S. Ackerman
Art historian, Harvard University

A miniature city and oversized house at the same time, Villa Adriana combines all the essential attributes of timeless architecture: the romantic ruin; the correspondence of building and landscape; the fundamental elements of construction—arch, wall, column; the "symphony" of ongoing accretion and renovation; and the considered syncopation, modulation, and sequence of space. And it's a great place for a picnic, too.
D. B. Middleton
Architect

I had the honor of excavating it when I was at the Academy in 1932. Mussolini visited the Academy and my studio and complimented me on my work.
Henry D. Mirick
Architect

ALSO RECOMMENDED BY
Pamela Starr, Roger B. Martin, Wayne Taylor

RECOMMENDED READING 17, 58, 84

To the mouth of the Tiber

You don't need a car to get to the mouth of the Tiber, but you do need several hours to spare, good walking shoes (or a bicycle), and protection against sunburn or windburn. Take the train from the Ostiense or Trastevere train station to Fiumicino Città. Walk across the via Portuense, look for the tall tower of the automobile drawbridge, and cross the Tiber Canal. This canal is an extension of one first built by the emperor Trajan as part of Portus, the ancient port of Rome (now several miles inland and a tourist attraction in its own right). Walking along the canal toward the sea, you will have a good view of the fishing boats, sailboats, and Coast Guard vessels that are the livelihood of the modern town of Fiumicino. The town center and church opposite you were designed by Giuseppe Valadier, who also created the neoclassical oval of Piazza del Popolo in Rome.

After passing the entrance to a footbridge, bear left and follow the main road (via Traiana) around the boat basin to the sea, where the road takes the name Lungomare della Salute. You can walk alongside the beach for several kilometers, keeping an old (inactive) lighthouse to your right. This is not a beautiful beach, but in the spring and summer, it is cheerful and crowded. Walk until the Lungomare ends, then continue along the beach until you see a sign for the restaurant Vecchia Scogliera. At this point the beach ends and you must walk along the road via del Faro. The lighthouse is still on your right, while white masts peeking over the horizon to your left hint at the presence of the Tiber ahead. This is a desolate landscape with few landmarks. After 10–15 minutes, you will reach an intersection; the road to the right leads to the lighthouse, the road to the left to a small shantytown of makeshift houses: a landscape made famous by Pier Paolo Pasolini. Take the road to the left for another 5–10 minutes, until the rock jetty is directly ahead of you. Climb a fishermen's ladder up the rocks and you will be at the mouth of the Tiber.

On the other side is Ostia, and both sides of the jetty are lined with fishing cranes and fisherman's nets. Sail-boats glide in and out of the river. About 100 meters further along the same road is an unpretentious but pleas-ant trattoria, Da Lilli, a good place to stop for a seafood lunch (closed Mondays). You will have walked about an hour from the center of Fiumicino, so allow about an hour to get back. Alternately, you can continue along the Tiber upstream until you reach an automobile bridge, where there is a bus stop. From here "Cotral" buses return to Fiumicino or cross the bridge to Ostia Lido.

In the summertime, an excursion boat runs from the automobile drawbridge in Fiumicino up the Tiber Canal to where it meets the Tiber, then down the river to its mouth. This guided tour (in Italian) is inexpensive and fun and take about two hours.

CHRISTINA HUEMER
Librarian, American Academy in Rome

Villa d'Este

built by Cardinal Ippolito d'Este II, mid-16th century
viale delle Cento Fontane, Tivoli,   ☎ 0774 31 20 70

See ancient and Renaissance statues and fountain sculpture
set into a garden design with a rich and lively iconography.
Especially in summer, go to enjoy the shade and fountains.
Kathryn Gleason
*Assistant professor of landscape architecture, Cornell
University, and co-principal investigator of the American
Academy in Rome excavation at Horace's Villa, Licenza*

After seeing Rome for several days, go to the Villa d'Este
one evening and stop before sundown at La Sibilla (via della
Sibilla 50,   ☎ 0774 20 281). Order a salad and chocolate
soufflé. Then go see the fountains at night (open until 11:30
p.m. in summer months).
Theodore Liebman
Architect

Villa d'Este's fountains are spectacular and unforgettable.
Jerome M. Cooper
Architect

RECOMMENDED READING 19, 53

OSTIA ANTICA

viale Romagnoli 717 (half hour by train from
Stazione Ostiense),   ☎ 06 565 00 22

Ostia Antica provides a glimpse of a Roman town with all the
typical buildings and areas—forum, streets, temples, houses
(both atrium-style and apartment houses, or tenements),
shops, statues, and inscriptions, and most impressive of all,
a theater facing the piazza of the "corporations" with mosaics
identifying the shopkeepers' specialties. Most enlightening
experience—to seek out the tiny shrines of Mithras hidden
among the narrow alleys.
Helen F. North
Classicist, Swarthmore College

Ostia provides the easiest and clearest way to understand
an ancient Roman town with a full range of building types,
including the bath complex excavated by Professor Frank
Brown which had such an enormous influence on Louis
Kahn's work.
George E. Hartman
Architect

One can still get lost in the skeletal remains of this abandoned
Roman port town. I prefer it to Pompeii.
Roger Ulrich
Classicist, Dartmouth College

Spectacular example of an ancient city—very manageable—
wonderful for a sunny spring or a summer day. Take a picnic
and just get lost there.
Katharine Brophy DuBois
Historian

ALSO RECOMMENDED BY
Lynn Kearney, Virginia Paquette, Leslie Rainer,
William O. Smith, Pamela Starr, Thomas H. Watkins

RECOMMENDED READING 66

✕ Mezza Luna

near Ostia Antica

A great place for warm days or evenings to enjoy a fish dinner. Greasy but lots of paper table covers to soak it up and
draw on, and a cheap meal. Like so much in Rome, finding
it is half the fun. Ask the guides at Ostia Antica for directions.
D. B. Middleton

EUR DISTRICT

Metro line "B" to the Fermi stop

For some reason EUR reminds me of Seaside, Florida. I see
it as a cautionary tale for architects, landscape architects,
and planners. American designers and planners should take

a break from photographing piazzas and visit the suburbs.
FREDERICK STEINER
Professor of planning and landscape architect, Arizona State University

EUR is an eccentric suggestion. See especially the Palazzo della Civiltà Italica (now del Lavoro) designed in 1925 by Giovanni Guerrini and others—a De Chirico setting in 3D. Also see the Museo della Civiltà Romana with the great *plastico* (scale model).
PETER J. HOLLIDAY
Historian of classical art and archaeology, California State University—Long Beach

RECOMMENDED READING 90, 91

Museo della Civiltà Romana

Piazza G. Agnelli 10, EUR,   ☎ 06 59 26 041

Mussolini's partly built permanent world's fair now houses a wonderful scale model of ancient Rome depicting the city in about the 3rd century AD. After wandering around the city and the Forum, it's worth a trip to EUR. In the same building are some wonderful (and more detailed) models of Roman buildings including a tenement, and a Pompeiian villa as well as some terrific architectural fragments. But the scale of the EUR complex is enormous, the distance from the Metro station is a veritable hike, and, typical of Italy, the museum's wonderful collection has poor, if any, explanatory notes and the guards know "nothin'."
BARRY LEWIS
Architectural historian

Plastico di Roma / Historical Model of Rome

This scale model shows the entire city of Rome as it existed during the height of Roman Imperial power. All of the present structures of Rome can be understood by studying this model. It is especially interesting to note how the Vatican and the great Renaissance and Baroque palaces were integrated later.
WALTER CHATHAM
Architect

Palazzo dei Congressi

Adalberto Libera, 1937
Piazza J.F. Kennedy (EUR)

Libera's convention center is possibly the finest monumental project produced in Italy between the wars. The collision of history, with its Imperial connotations, and the modern, with its progressive drive, pushed Libera to radical gestures in a project that was begun in 1937, interrupted by the war, and finally completed in 1952. A colonnade of the obligatory EUR columns faces the piazza but behind and separate from it is a vast glass wall stabilized by arching trusses. The two do not harmonize. Note the strip of windows along the side and the massive vaulted cube of the convention hall that thrusts up from the marble body of the building. The roof theater was the set for the madhouse in Bertolucci's 1970 film *The Conformist*.

MICHAEL STANTON
Architect

San Paolo alle Tre Fontane

5th century, rebuilt by Giacomo Della Porta, 1599
off viale Cristoforo Colombo (near EUR)

Saint Paul was allegedly beheaded here and three springs marked the place where his head supposedly bounced three times. A unique palimpsest of 13th- to 16th-century buildings in a park (inside a Trappist monastery); note the "portrait" of the Monte Argentario in the vault of the gate tower. Very suggestive ambience.

ELFRIEDE AND GEORG KNAUER
Consulting scholar, University Museum, University of Pennsylvania; Classicist, University of Pennsylvania

FORO ITALICO AND VICINITY

Stadio dei Marmi

Enrico Del Debbio, 1928–1935
Piazza del Foro Italico

This, like much architecture of the Fascist era, is good but
ignored.
PETER J. HOLLIDAY
*Historian of classical art and archaeology, California State
University-Long Beach*

Palestra di Scherma

Luigi Moretti, 1936
Piazza del Foro Italico

The Fencing Academy's elegant marble-clad building was
designed to celebrate physical culture at the 1936 Olympics.
After the war, the building fell into disrepair. It was used
for the Red Brigade trials in the 1970s because of its fortress-
like qualities and protected location. It illustrates the way
that many 20th-century buildings are already becoming the
next layer of ruins in Rome.
WALTER CHATHAM
Architect

This building is one of several in Rome by my favorite modern Italian architect. I admire it for its combination of
functional modern sculptural forms clad in subtly detailed
white marble, referencing classical Roman buildings.
ROBERT EVANS
Architect

Villa Madama

*Raphael, 1516; continued by Antonio da Sangallo and
by Giulio Romano*
via Villa Madama near Foro Italico
Admission by special arrangement

Depicts a clear relationship between a building and its

designed landscape, in contrast to its surrounding environ-
ment. Decorated with friezes and stuccoes by Giulio Romano.
JEROME M. COOPER
Architect

FARTHER AFIELD

✗ ## Da Mastino

Fregene, 20–30 minutes from Rome

The most wonderful, lively, relaxed, elegant, informal *ristorante/
stabilimento* and beachfront I remember. In the summer,
it's an afternoon-long tour of Roman cuisine and culture.
RICHARD ROTH

Palazzo Colonna Barberini / Museo Nazionale Archaeologico Prenestino

Palestrina, 1 hour by train from Rome

The palace, built over the site of an extensive tiered Temple
of Fortune, houses one of the great unsung artistic treasures
in the world: the 1st-century BC Nile Mosaic. Taken from
the ruins of the forum of the Roman city of Praeneste, this
depiction of the Nile landscape measures some twenty by
fifteen feet, populated by animals, priestesses, and the
flooded river.
PAMELA STARR
Music historian, University of Nebraska

Ninfa

48 miles southeast of Rome, near the town of
Norma, in the Caetani Botanical Gardens
☎ 06 68 80 32 31

Visit a ruined medieval-Renaissance town. Ninfa was abandoned in the 17th century because of a malaria epidemic. In
the surrounding Villa Caetani Botanical Gardens, there is a

lake and canals bordered by lavender. Though the park is only opened to the public on the first weekend of each month, Ninfa's serene atmosphere is worth the trouble and distance. In Sermoneta, above Ninfa, is a restaurant famous for its pasta.

Robert Hamilton
Painter

Sanctuary of Feronia / Lucus Feroniae

c. 50 BC
20 miles north of Rome, on Autostrada A1
☎ 06 908 51 73

The sanctuary of Feronia is an interesting site—an old shrine with a late-Republican commercial area attached to it—that one never thinks to visit. It is close to Rome, very near a tiny town called Fiano Romano—the last Tiber port before Rome. There's a castlelike structure that I don't associate with Italy at all. Lucus Feroniae is only open two days per week and no one goes there so the site is immaculate and the custodian walks you around and chats. Very pleasant.

Anne Weis
Art historian, University of Pittsburgh

RECOMMENDED READING 18

Cerveteri

10th–4th century BC
1+ hour from Rome, by train,   ☎ 06 09 94 1354

This ancient Etruscan necropolis is like a mini-Rome built by the precursors to the Romans. It is entirely made of carved tufa, a soft volcanic stone, and appears to link Roman and Hellenic culture back to the Stone Age—and forward to the present.

Walter Chatham
Architect

Tarquinia

2+ hours from Rome, by train

Go to Tarquinia (and Cerveteri) to see Etruscan tombs, frescoes, vases, and sculpture.

JOHN KEARNEY

Sculptor

INDEX OF
RECOMMENDED READING

INDEX BY CONTRIBUTOR

GENERAL INDEX

Index of Recommended Reading

1. James S. Ackerman, *The Architecture of Michelangelo*, University of Chicago Press, 1986.

2. P. Aicher, *Guide to the Aqueducts of Rome*, Bolchazy Carducci, 1995.

3. T. Ashby, *Aqueducts of Ancient Rome*, o.p.

4. Marcus Aurelius, *The Meditations of Marcus Aurelius*, Avon, 1993.

5. Jonathan Barnett, *The Elusive City: Five Centuries of Design, Ambition and Miscalculation*, o.p.

6. Anthony Blunt, *A Guide to Baroque Rome*, o.p.

7. Mary Taliaferro Boatwright, *Hadrian and the City of Rome*, Princeton University Press, 1989.

8. Larissa Bonfante, *Etruscan Life and Afterlife: A Handbook of Etruscan Studies*, Wayne State University Press, 1987.

9. Bruce Boucher, *The Sculpture of Jacopo Sansovino*, Yale University Press, 1992.

10. Steven Brooke, *Views of Rome*, Rizzoli, 1995.

11. George Bull, *Michelangelo: A Biography*, St. Martin's, 1998.

12. Jacob Burckhardt, *The Civilization of the Renaissance in Italy*, Penguin USA, 1990.

13. Giovanni Careri, *Bernini: Flights of Love, the Art of Devotion*, University of Chicago Press, 1995.

14. David Castriota, *The Ara Pacis Augustae and the Imagery of Abundance in Later Greek and Early Roman Imperial Art*, Princeton University Press, 1995.

15. Benvenuto Cellini, *The Autobiography of Benvenuto Cellini*, Viking, 1956.

16. Amanda Claridge, *Rome: An Oxford Archaeological Guide*, Oxford University Press, 1998.

17. Eleanor Clark, *Rome and a Villa*, Atheneum, 1962, o.p.

18. Filippo Coarelli, *Rome (Monuments of Civilization)*, o.p.

19. David R. Coffin, *The Villa in the Life of Renaissance Rome*, Princeton University Press, 1988.

20. Joseph Connors, *Borromini and the Roman Oratory: Style and Society*, o.p.

21. Alessandro Cruciani, *Roma e Dintorni: Guida d'Italia del Touring Club Italiano*, 7th edition, TCI, 1977.

47. Henry James, *Portrait of a Lady*.

48. Waldemar Januszczak, *Sayonara, Michelangelo: The Sistine Chapel Restored and Repackaged*, o.p.

49. B. Jatta, ed., *Piranesi e l'Aventino* (exhibition catalog), Rome, 1998.

50. John Keats, "The Eve of St. Agnes" in *Collected Poems of John Keats*.

51. Richard Krautheimer, *Rome: Profile of a City*, Princeton University Press, 1980.

52. Irving Lavin, *Bernini and the Unity of the Visual Arts* (Vols. I and II), Oxford University Press, 1980, o.p.

53. Claudia Lazzaro, *Italian Renaissance Gardens: From the Conventions of Planting, Design, and Ornament to the Grand Gardens of Sixteenth-Century Central Italy*, o.p.

54. James Less-Milne, *St. Peter's*, o.p.

55. Paul Letarouilly, *Vatican and the Basilica of St. Peter*.

56. Alexander Liberman and Joseph Brodsky, *Campidoglio: Michelangelo's Roman Capitol*, Random House, 1994.

57. William L. MacDonald, *The Architecture of the Roman Empire: An Introductory Study*, Vols. I and II, Yale University Press, 1982.

58. William L. MacDonald, John A. Pinto, Henry McBride, *Hadrian's Villa and Its Legacy*, Yale University Press, 1997.

59. William L. MacDonald, *Pantheon: Design, Meaning and Progeny*, Harvard University Press, 1981.

60. Alta Macadam, *The Blue Guide: Rome and Environs*, 6th edition, W. W. Norton, 1998.

61. Rowland Mainstone, *Developments in Structural Form*, Butterworth Architecture, 1998.

62. Tod A. Marder, *Bernini and the Art of Architecture*, Cambridge University Press, 1998.

63. John Rupert Martin, *Baroque*, Harper and Row, 1977.

64. Georgina Masson, *The Companion Guide to Rome* (revised by Tim Jepson), Companion Guides, 1998.

65. Thomas F. Mathews, *The Clash of Gods: A Reinterpretation of Early Christian Art*, Princeton University Press, 1995.

66. Russell Meiggs, *Roman Ostia*, Oxford University Press, 1980.

67. H. A. Millon, "The Antamoro Chapel in S. Girolamo della Carita," in *Studies in Italian Art and Architecture*, American Academy in Rome, 1980.

68. Harry Mulisch, *The Discovery of Heaven*, (Paul Vincent, trans.), Penguin, 1997.

69. Nash, *The Pictorial Dictionary of Ancient Rome*, o.p.

70. Norman Neuerburg, *L'Architettura delle Fontane e dei Ninfei nell'Italia Antica*, Napoli: Gaetano Macchiaroli Editore.

71. Ovid, *Metamorphoses*.

72. Iain Pears, *The Bernini Bust*, Harcourt Brace, 1994.

73. Iain Pears, *Death and Restoration*, Scribner, 1998.

74. Iain Pears, *Giotto's Hand*, o.p.

75. Iain Pears, *The Last Judgement*, Scribner, 1996.

76. Iain Pears, *The Raphael Affair*, Penguin USA, 1998.

77. Iain Pears, *The Titian Committee*, Penguin USA, 1999.

78. Carlo Pietrangeli, Michael Hirst, Gianluigi Colalucci, Fabrizio Mancinelli, John Shearman, *The Sistine Chapel: A Glorious Restoration*, Abrams, 1994.

79. J. Pollitt, *Art in the Hellenistic Age*, Cambridge University Press, 1986.

80. Catherine Puglisi, *Caravaggio*, Phaidon, 1998.

81. Laure Raffaelli, *The Knopf Guide to Rome*, Knopf, 1994.

82. Ottorino Respighi, *Fontane di Roma/Pini di Roma/Feste Romane*, Philadelphia Orchestra, Eugene Ormandy, (CD).

83. L. Richardson, *A New Topographical Dictionary of Ancient Rome*, Johns Hopkins University Press, 1992.

84. Colin Rowe, *Collage City*, MIT Press, 1984.

85. Ingrid Rowland, *Culture of the High Renaissance*, Cambridge University Press, 1998.

86. John Ruskin, *The Seven Lamps of Architecture*, 1849.

87. John Belden Scott, *Images of Nepotism: The Paintings of Palazzo Barberini*, Princeton University Press, 1991.

88. Percy Bysshe Shelley, *The Cenci: A Tragedy in Five Acts*, 1819.

89. Richard Spear, *Domenichino*, Yale University Press, 1983, o.p.

90. Albert Speer, *Inside the Third Reich*, Touchstone Books, 1997.

91. Albert Speer, *The Secret Spandau Diaries*, o.p.

92. Leo Steinberg, *Borromini's San Carlo Alle Quatro Fontane: A Study in Multiple Form and Architectural Symbolism*, o.p.

93. Stendhal, *Rome, Naples Et Florence*, Schoenhof Foreign Books, translated by Haakon Chevalier, Collier, 1961, 1988.

94. Alexander Stille, *Benevolence and Betrayal*, Penguin, 1993.

95. Suetonius, *Lives of the Caesars*, Loeb Classical Library, Harvard University Press.

96. Marilyn Symmes and Kenneth Breisch, eds., *Fountains: Splash and Spectacle*, Rizzoli, 1998.

97. Tacitus, *The Annals of Imperial Rome*, Loeb Classical Library, Harvard University Press.

98. M. Torelli, G. Pianu, *M. Morella Etruria Meridionale: Southern Etruria*, Oxford University Press, 1994.

99. William L. Vance, *America's Rome: Catholic and Contemporary Rome*, Yale University Press, 1989.

100. William L. Vance, *America's Rome: Classical Rome*, Yale University Press, 1989.

101. John Varriano, *Italian Baroque and Rococo Architecture* Oxford University Press, 1986.

102. John Varriano, *A Literary Companion to Rome*, St. Martin's, 1995.

103. Giorgio Vasari, *The Lives of the Artists*, Oxford University Press, 1998.

104. Francesco Venturi and Mario Sanfilippo, *Fountains of Rome*, Vendome, 1996.

105. William Wallace, *Michelangelo: The Complete Sculpture, Painting, Architecture*.

106. J. M. Wallace-Hadrill, *Barbarian West: The Early Middle Ages, A.D. 400-1000*, o.p.

107. Stefanie Walker and Frederick Hammond, *Life and the Arts in the Baroque Palaces of Rome*, Yale University Press, 1999.

108. John B. Ward-Perkins, *Roman Imperial Architecture*, 2nd edition, Penguin Books, 1981.

109. Edith Wharton, *Roman Fever*.

110. John White, *The Birth and Rebirth of Pictorial Space*, o.p.

111. J. Wilton-Ely, *Piranesi as Architect and Designer*, Yale University Press, 1993.

112. Rudolf Wittkower, *Art and Architecture in Italy: 1600-1750 (Pelican History of Art)*, Yale University Press, 1992.

113. Rudolf Wittkower, *Bernini: The Sculptor of the Roman Baroque*, Phaidon, 1997.

114. Fikret Yegul, *Baths and Bathing in Classical Antiquity*, MIT Press, 1996.

115. Marguerite Yourcenar, *Memoirs of Hadrian*, Noonday Press/Farrar, Straus and Giroux, 1951, 1990.

116. John Pinto, Nolli map website, www.princeton.edu/almagest/nollimap.html

Index by Contributor

A

B

General Index

SPECIAL SALES

Little Bookroom publications are available at special discounts for bulk purchases for sales promotions or premiums. Special editions, including personalized covers, excerpts of existing guides, and corporate imprints, can be created in large quantities for special needs. For more information, contact The Little Bookroom, 5 St. Luke's Place, New York NY 10014. Inquiries from the United Kingdom and European Community should be sent to Granta Books, 2/3 Hanover Yard, Noel Road, London N1 8BE.

City Secrets: Rome combines the use of the Bell Gothic and Filosofia typefaces. The main text is set in Filosofia, a modern, somewhat geometric interpretation of the classic Bodoni. The highly legible Bell Gothic, used in various headings throughout the book, provides a fastidious contrast to the stylish Filosofia.

The American Academy in Rome, a center for independent study and advanced research in the arts and humanities, is located on the Janiculum, the highest point within the walls of Rome. For the scores of artists, art historians, classicists, architects, and writers who have been awarded a Rome Prize, "the beauty and resources of the place, the quality and variety of the friendships, the depth of Rome, and the time and freedom to work," mark their stay there as among the top two or three experiences of a lifetime.

Fellows, Residents, Visitors, and friends of the American Academy have generously shared their personal and professional insights in *City Secrets: Rome*. A portion of the proceeds from the sale of this guide will help support the Academy's ongoing programs.

NOTES

NOTES

NOTES